Profitable Strategies:

A Comprehensive Guide to Understanding the Fundamentals of Stock Trading with Equip yourself, knowledge and confidence to earn money in the Share Market

Lewis Finan

Table of Contents

Introduction

In today's dynamic financial landscape, the stock market stands as a realm of both unprecedented opportunity and inherent risk. For individuals seeking to harness the potential of this intricate market, knowledge becomes the cornerstone of success. Welcome to "Profitable Strategies," a comprehensive guide meticulously crafted to demystify the fundamentals of stock trading, empowering you to navigate the complexities of the share market with competence and confidence.

Embarking on a journey through the pages of this book, you'll find yourself equipped with a robust understanding of the principles that underpin stock trading. Whether you're a novice investor taking your first steps or a seasoned trader looking to refine your strategies, this guide offers insights that cater to all levels of expertise.

From the very basics of what stocks are and how they function within the market ecosystem, to the more advanced concepts of technical and fundamental analysis, "Profitable Strategies" covers a spectrum of topics designed to build your foundational knowledge. You'll unravel the significance of market trends, decipher the intricacies of reading stock charts, and comprehend how economic indicators influence stock prices.

But this guide is more than a mere compilation of theories – it's a hands-on manual. Dive into real-world case studies that illustrate both successful and cautionary tales from the stock market's annals. Learn how to identify high-potential stocks, manage risk effectively, and make informed decisions based on a blend of analysis and intuition.

As you progress through these pages, you'll find clarity on various trading styles, allowing you to tailor your approach to match your personality, risk tolerance, and financial goals. Swing trading, day trading, value investing – each strategy is dissected to provide you with a comprehensive overview, helping you identify the approach that resonates best with your aspirations.

But knowledge alone isn't enough; confidence is the key that unlocks the doors to success. "Profitable Strategies" is designed not only to educate but also to instill the confidence necessary to navigate the ever-changing landscape of the share market. Armed with insights, backed by historical perspectives, and supported by a rich array of resources, you'll be poised to make calculated moves that position you for potential profits.

Whether you're an individual investor seeking financial independence or someone looking to supplement their income through strategic trading, this guide is your companion in the intricate world of stock trading. By the time you turn the last page, you'll not only grasp the language of the market but also possess the tools to harness its potential. Let "Profitable Strategies" be your beacon as you embark on your journey to earning money in the captivating realm of the share market.

The Importance of Profitable Stock Trading

Profitable stock trading serves as a pivotal cornerstone within the realm of finance, offering individuals and businesses alike an avenue to accumulate wealth, achieve financial goals, and participate in the growth of companies and economies. The importance of this practice transcends mere financial gain; it intersects with the broader dynamics of global markets, personal financial well-being, and the broader economy. Here's a closer look at why profitable stock trading holds such immense significance:

- **Wealth Accumulation and Financial Goals**: For individual investors, profitable stock trading provides a pathway to accumulate wealth over time. By making informed decisions and capitalizing on market opportunities, investors can witness their initial investments grow substantially. This wealth accumulation can serve various purposes, from securing retirement funds to funding major life milestones, such as education, homeownership, or travel.

- **Capital Formation for Companies**: The stock market offers companies a means to raise capital by issuing shares to the public. Investors who purchase these shares provide companies with the necessary funds for expansion, research and development, and other growth-oriented endeavors. Profitable stock trading incentivizes individuals to invest in companies, fostering economic growth and job creation.

- **Market Efficiency**: The pursuit of profit drives investors to assess companies' performance meticulously. Profitable stock trading encourages due diligence, research, and the evaluation of financial indicators. These practices contribute to market efficiency by ensuring that stock prices are reflective of a company's actual performance, reducing information asymmetry.

- **Economic Indicators**: The movement of stock prices can serve as a barometer for the broader economic health of a nation. Rising stock prices may indicate confidence in economic prospects while declining prices can signal concerns. Thus, profitable stock trading can offer insights into the overall economic sentiment.

- **Innovation and Entrepreneurship**: The stock market rewards innovation and entrepreneurship. Companies with promising products or groundbreaking ideas often attract investor interest, leading to capital infusion. This not only benefits the companies but also spurs innovation and progress across various industries.

- **Global Financial Markets**: Profitable stock trading contributes to the functioning of global financial markets. Investors from around the world participate in trading, creating a diverse marketplace that facilitates the flow of capital across borders. This interconnectedness fosters international economic cooperation and growth.

- **Personal Financial Empowerment**: Learning the art of profitable stock trading empowers individuals with financial literacy and independence. It equips them with the skills to make informed decisions about their investments, understand market trends, and manage risk effectively.
- **Long-Term Wealth Creation**: Profitable stock trading isn't just about short-term gains. It can also play a significant role in long-term wealth creation. Patient and strategic investment choices can lead to compounding returns over time, helping individuals secure their financial futures.
- **Economic Resilience**: A well-functioning stock market contributes to economic resilience. During periods of economic uncertainty, companies with solid fundamentals and growth potential can weather downturns, benefiting both investors and the broader economy.

In essence, profitable stock trading isn't merely a pursuit of financial gains; it's a practice that fuels economic growth, fosters innovation, and empowers individuals to take charge of their financial destinies. Its importance reverberates through personal aspirations, corporate ambitions, and the interconnected fabric of global economies.

Setting the Stage for Success

Success, in any endeavor, is often a culmination of meticulous planning, diligent preparation, and a resolute commitment to one's goals. When it comes to ventures as dynamic and intricate as stock trading, the foundation upon which success is built becomes even more crucial. "Setting the Stage for Success" in the world of stock trading entails a series of strategic steps and mindset adjustments that pave the way for informed decisions, calculated risks, and ultimately, profitable outcomes.

- **Educational Foundation**: Like any craft, successful stock trading begins with education. Before diving into the complexities of the market, aspiring traders should dedicate time to learning about the fundamentals of stocks, market dynamics, and trading strategies. Acquiring a solid educational foundation arms traders with the knowledge needed to decipher market trends, interpret financial indicators, and make informed decisions.
- **Clear Objectives**: Defining clear and achievable objectives is paramount. Are you looking for short-term gains, long-term investments, or a mix of both? Setting specific financial goals guides your trading approach and risk tolerance. Having a well-defined purpose keeps you focused and prevents impulsive decisions driven by market fluctuations.
- **Risk Management**: Success in stock trading hinges on effective risk management. Establishing a risk-reward ratio for each trade helps you protect your capital. Diversification – spreading investments across different stocks or sectors – is another crucial element of risk management. It reduces the impact of a single stock's poor performance on your overall portfolio.
- **Mindset and Discipline**: The psychology of trading plays a pivotal role. Emotions can cloud judgment and lead to irrational decisions. Cultivating a disciplined mindset involves acknowledging the potential for losses, staying patient during market fluctuations, and adhering to a well-defined trading plan.

- **Trading Plan**: A meticulously crafted trading plan acts as your roadmap to success. It outlines your goals, strategies, risk management approach, and criteria for entering and exiting trades. Following a trading plan helps you avoid making decisions based on impulse, which can be detrimental in the fast-paced world of trading.

- **Continuous Learning**: The stock market is dynamic, and staying current is essential. Regularly seek out new information, stay updated on market trends, and adapt your strategies accordingly. Learning from both successes and mistakes helps refine your approach over time.

- **Technical and Fundamental Analysis**: Proficiency in technical and fundamental analysis is crucial. Technical analysis involves studying stock price patterns and charts to predict future price movements. Fundamental analysis entails evaluating a company's financial health and growth potential. A balanced understanding of both methods enhances your decision-making ability.

- **Patience and Resilience**: Stock trading isn't a get-rich-quick scheme. Patience is key. Some trades may yield rapid returns, while others require time to mature. Embrace losses as learning experiences and remain resilient in the face of setbacks.

- **Adaptability**: Markets evolve, and your strategies should too. Stay open to adapting your approach as market conditions change. Flexibility allows you to capitalize on emerging opportunities and navigate challenges effectively.

- **Utilizing Technology**: Embrace technological tools that facilitate research, analysis, and trading execution. Online platforms, research software, and trading apps can streamline your trading process and provide real-time insights.

"Setting the Stage for Success" in stock trading is a multifaceted endeavor. It blends knowledge, discipline, strategy, and a growth-oriented mindset. By meticulously preparing the groundwork, aspiring traders position themselves to navigate the complexities of the stock market with confidence, and ultimately, to reap the rewards of their endeavors.

Chapter 1: Understanding Stock Market Fundamentals

The stock market stands as a dynamic arena where companies issue shares, and investor's trade these shares, all with the aim of achieving financial goals. Beneath the surface of this bustling marketplace lies a series of fundamental concepts that shape its functioning and influence investment decisions. In this comprehensive exploration, we delve into the key elements of stock market fundamentals, unraveling the intricate web that underpins this vital facet of the global economy.

1. Stocks and Shares: The Building Blocks of Ownership

At the heart of the stock market are stocks, also known as shares or equities. These represent ownership stakes in a company. When an individual purchases shares, they become a shareholder, entitling them to a portion of the company's assets and earnings. Shares can be categorized into common and preferred, each with its own set of rights and privileges.

2. Market Exchanges: The Trading Platforms

Stocks are bought and sold on stock exchanges, which serve as platforms for trading. Major exchanges like the New York Stock Exchange (NYSE) and NASDAQ provide the infrastructure for buyers and sellers to interact. Here, the forces of supply and demand determine stock prices in a continuous auction-like process.

3. Market Indices: Gauges of Market Performance

Indices, such as the S&P 500 and Dow Jones Industrial Average, aggregate the performance of a group of stocks to provide insights into the overall market's direction. Investors often use these indices as benchmarks to assess the performance of their portfolios and the broader market.

4. Market Capitalization: Sizing Up Companies

Market capitalization, or market cap, measures a company's value by multiplying its stock price by the number of outstanding shares. It classifies companies as large-cap, mid-cap, or small-cap, offering investors a sense of the company's size and potential growth trajectory.

5. Price-to-Earnings (P/E) Ratio: Valuing Stocks

The P/E ratio is a fundamental metric used to evaluate a company's valuation. It compares the stock's price to its earnings per share (EPS), indicating how much investors are willing to pay for a dollar of earnings. A higher P/E may suggest growth expectations, while a lower ratio could indicate undervaluation.

6. Dividends: The Investor's Reward

Dividends are periodic payments made by companies to their shareholders from their profits. Dividend yield, calculated by dividing the annual dividend by the stock price, is a measure of the income a stock generates for its investors. Companies that pay dividends often attract income-focused investors.

7. Earnings Per Share (EPS): Profit Allocation

EPS measures a company's profitability by dividing its earnings by the number of outstanding shares. It is a crucial factor in determining a company's valuation and growth potential. Rising EPS often reflects favorable business performance.

8. Fundamental vs. Technical Analysis: Different Approaches

Investors employ two main methods to analyze stocks: fundamental and technical analysis. Fundamental analysis assesses a company's financial health, management quality, industry trends, and more. Technical analysis, on the other hand, examines price charts and patterns to predict future price movements.

9. Market Trends: Bull and Bear Markets

Market trends play a significant role in stock trading. A bull market is characterized by rising prices and investor optimism, while a bear market involves falling prices and pessimism. Understanding these trends helps investors make informed decisions and manage risk.

10. Economic Indicators: Linking Markets and Economy

Economic indicators, such as GDP growth, unemployment rates, and consumer spending, impact stock markets. Positive economic data can boost investor confidence and drive stock prices upward, while negative indicators may trigger market declines.

11. Investment Strategies: The Diverse Approaches

Investors employ various strategies, such as value investing, growth investing, and income investing, to achieve their financial goals. Value investors seek undervalued stocks, growth investors target companies with strong growth potential, and income investor's focus on dividend-paying stocks.

12. Risk Management: Mitigating Potential Losses

Risk management is a critical aspect of successful stock trading. Diversification, setting stop-loss orders, and understanding a company's financials are strategies to manage risk and protect investment capital.

13. Behavioral Finance: Psychology in Investing

Behavioral finance studies how psychological biases influence investment decisions. Emotions like fear and greed can lead to irrational choices, impacting trading outcomes. Recognizing these biases helps investors make more objective decisions.

14. Global Markets: An Interconnected Landscape

In today's globalized world, stock markets are interconnected. News, events, and economic shifts in one part of the world can have ripple effects across other markets. Understanding these linkages is essential for making informed cross-border investment decisions.

15. Long-Term Perspective: The Power of Compounding

A long-term perspective is crucial for harnessing the full potential of the stock market. Compounding returns over time can lead to substantial wealth accumulation. Staying invested through market fluctuations and being patient are keys to reaping these rewards.

In conclusion, delving into the world of stock market fundamentals unveils a tapestry woven from various threads of knowledge and strategy. From understanding the essence of ownership through shares to grasping the intricacies of valuation metrics and investment strategies, these fundamentals empower investors to navigate the ever-evolving landscape of stock trading. By comprehending the interplay of economics, psychology, and data analysis, individuals can position themselves to make informed decisions and harness the potential of the stock market for their financial growth and security.

1.1 What is a Stock?

A stock, often referred to as a share or equity, represents ownership in a company. It signifies a fractional ownership interest in the company's assets, earnings, and future growth. When individuals or institutional investors purchase stocks, they become shareholders, entitling them to certain rights and benefits. Understanding the concept of stocks is fundamental to comprehend how the stock market operates and how investors participate in the world of corporate ownership and investment. Here are important points that elucidate the concept of stocks:

1. **Ownership Stake**: Stocks represent a slice of ownership in a company. When an individual owns shares in a company, they hold a portion of the company's total ownership. The percentage of ownership depends on the number of shares owned relative to the total number of outstanding shares.
2. **Voting Rights**: Shareholders often have the right to vote on certain company decisions, such as the appointment of board members and major business transactions. The number of votes is generally proportional to the number of shares held, granting larger shareholders greater influence.
3. **Dividends**: Some companies distribute a portion of their profits to shareholders in the form of dividends. Dividends are usually paid on a regular basis and provide an additional stream of income for investors. Dividend payments depend on the company's financial performance and its dividend policy.
4. **Capital Appreciation**: One of the main reasons investors buy stocks is the potential for capital appreciation. If the company performs well and its value increases, the stock price may rise, allowing investors to sell their shares at a higher price than they paid, thereby realizing a profit.
5. **Types of Stocks**: There are common stocks and preferred stocks. Common stocks offer voting rights and the potential for dividends and capital gains. Preferred stocks, while usually offering a fixed dividend, often lack voting rights. In the event of bankruptcy,

preferred shareholders are generally paid before common shareholders.

6. **Initial Public Offering (IPO)**: When a company decides to go public and issue shares to the general public for the first time, it conducts an IPO. This is a significant event in a company's lifecycle and can attract substantial investor attention.

7. **Secondary Market Trading**: After an IPO, stocks are traded on secondary markets like stock exchanges. Buyers and sellers interact in these markets, determining the stock's price based on supply and demand.

8. **Ticker Symbols**: Stocks are identified by ticker symbols, short codes used for trading purposes. These symbols help investors easily track and trade stocks on exchanges.

9. **Market Capitalization**: The market capitalization of a company is calculated by multiplying its stock price by the total number of outstanding shares. It represents the company's total value as perceived by the market and categorizes companies into various size categories, such as large-cap, mid-cap, and small-cap.

10. **Risks and Rewards**: Investing in stocks carries inherent risks and rewards. The potential for higher returns comes with the risk of price volatility and potential losses. Diversification and research are strategies used to manage risks and make informed investment decisions.

11. **Indices and Portfolios**: Indices, such as the S&P 500 or NASDAQ, group together stocks to represent the overall market's performance. Investors often create portfolios, a collection of different stocks, to achieve diversification and manage risk.

12. **Long-Term Perspective**: While stock prices can be influenced by short-term market fluctuations, many investors adopt a long-term perspective. Over time, the stock market has historically shown an upward trajectory, reflecting the growth of economies and companies.

In essence, a stock represents ownership in a company and offers investors the potential for financial gains through capital appreciation and dividends. By understanding the nuances of stocks and their role in the broader financial landscape, individuals can make informed investment decisions, participate in corporate ownership, and potentially achieve their financial goals.

1.2 How the Stock Market Works

The stock market, a dynamic and intricate financial ecosystem, serves as a platform where investors buy and sell shares of publicly traded companies. This marketplace is driven by the interplay of supply and demand, influenced by a myriad of factors ranging from economic indicators to investor sentiment. Understanding how the stock market functions is essential for investors seeking to navigate its complexities and capitalize on investment opportunities. Here's a comprehensive overview of how the stock market works:

1. **Companies Go Public: The IPO Process**

The journey begins when a privately held company decides to go public and issue shares to the public for the first time. This process is known as an Initial Public Offering (IPO). During an IPO, the company's shares are listed on a stock exchange, allowing investors to buy and sell them.

2. **Secondary Market Trading: Buying and Selling Shares**

Once a company's shares are listed on an exchange, they can be traded on the secondary market. Buyers and sellers interact on the exchange, determining the stock's price through the forces of supply and demand. The secondary market is where most stock trading takes place and where investors can enter or exit positions.

3.   Stock Exchanges and Over-the-Counter (OTC) Markets

Stock exchanges, such as the New York Stock Exchange (NYSE) and NASDAQ, provide the infrastructure for organized trading. They facilitate the buying and selling of stocks through a regulated and transparent process. Over-the-counter (OTC) markets, on the other hand, operate without a centralized exchange. OTC stocks are often traded electronically, and they include stocks of smaller companies that may not meet the requirements for listing on major exchanges.

4.   Stock Symbols and Ticker Codes

Each publicly traded company is identified by a stock symbol or ticker code, which is a short combination of letters used to uniquely identify the stock. Ticker symbols make it easier for investors to track and trade stocks.

5.   Bid and Ask Prices: The Price Differential

In stock trading, there are two key prices: the bid price and the ask price. The bid price represents the highest price that a buyer is willing to pay for a stock, while the ask price is the lowest price at which a seller is willing to sell. The difference between these prices is known as the bid-ask spread.

6. Market Orders and Limit Orders

Investors place orders to buy or sell stocks. A market order instructs the broker to execute the trade at the best available price. A limit order specifies the maximum price a buyer is willing to pay or the minimum price a seller is willing to accept.

7. Market Indices: Gauging Overall Market Performance

Market indices, like the S&P 500 or Dow Jones Industrial Average, track the performance of a specific group of stocks. These indices serve as benchmarks for assessing the overall direction of the market.

8. Fundamental and Technical Analysis

Investors employ different analysis methods to make informed decisions. Fundamental analysis involves evaluating a company's financial health, industry trends, and management quality. Technical analysis, on the other hand, studies price charts and patterns to predict future price movements.

9. Economic Indicators and Market Impact

Economic indicators, such as GDP growth, inflation rates, and unemployment figures, influence market sentiment and stock prices. Positive indicators often lead to market optimism, while negative indicators can trigger market declines.

10. Investor Sentiment and Market Trends

Investor sentiment plays a significant role in driving market trends. Positive news can lead to bullish trends, with rising prices and increased buying activity. Negative news can result in bearish trends, marked by falling prices and heightened selling activity.

11. Long-Term Investment and Short-Term Trading

Investors adopt various strategies, including long-term investing and short-term trading. Long-term investors seek to capitalize on the market's overall growth over time, while short-term traders aim to profit from price fluctuations in the near term.

12. Regulatory Oversight and Investor Protection

Stock markets are regulated to ensure fair and transparent trading. Regulatory bodies, such as the U.S. Securities and Exchange Commission (SEC), enforce rules that protect investors from fraudulent activities and maintain market integrity.

In essence, the stock market is a dynamic arena where investors and traders interact to buy and sell shares of publicly traded companies. It's influenced by a multitude of factors, from economic indicators to investor sentiment, and serves as a barometer of economic health and corporate performance. Understanding how the stock market functions empowers individuals to make informed investment decisions, manage risk, and participate in the ever-evolving landscape of finance.

1.3 Types of Stocks

In the realm of investing, stocks come in various forms, each with distinct characteristics, benefits, and considerations. Understanding the types of stocks is essential for investors to tailor their portfolios to their financial goals and risk preferences. Here's a comprehensive overview of the different types of stocks:

1. Common Stocks: Ownership and Growth Potential

Common stocks are the most prevalent type of stock. When investors purchase common shares, they become partial owners of the company and are entitled to a portion of its profits and assets. Common shareholders also have voting rights in certain company decisions, such as electing board members. Common stocks offer the potential for capital appreciation over time, making them popular among growth-oriented investors.

2. Preferred Stocks: Dividends and Priority

Preferred stocks, as the name suggests, hold certain preferences over common stocks. Preferred shareholders have a higher claim on the company's assets and earnings compared to common shareholders. They often receive fixed dividend payments, which are distributed before dividends are paid to common shareholders. However, preferred shareholders usually do not have voting rights.

3. Growth Stocks: Capital Appreciation Focus

Growth stocks belong to companies that are expected to experience above-average earnings growth compared to other companies in the market. These companies often reinvest their earnings to fuel expansion and innovation, rather than distributing dividends. Investors are attracted to growth stocks for their potential to appreciate significantly in value over time, although they typically carry higher volatility and risk.

4. Value Stocks: Undervalued Investments

Value stocks are shares of companies that appear to be trading at a price lower than their intrinsic value. These companies may be temporarily undervalued due to market sentiment or industry trends. Value investors seek such opportunities, believing that the stock's price will eventually reflect the company's true worth, leading to potential gains.

5. Dividend Stocks: Income Generation

Dividend stocks are shares of companies that regularly distribute a portion of their profits as dividends to shareholders. These stocks are favored by income-focused investors who seek a consistent stream of passive income. Dividend-paying companies are often established and stable, making them attractive to those looking for more predictable returns.

6. Blue-Chip Stocks: Established Leaders

Blue-chip stocks refer to shares of well-established, financially stable companies with a history of strong performance. These companies are leaders in their industries, often household names, and are known for their resilience even during economic downturns. Blue-chip stocks are favored by conservative investors seeking stability and long-term growth potential.

7. Small-Cap, Mid-Cap, and Large-Cap Stocks: Company Size Categories

Stocks are often categorized based on market capitalization:

- **Small-Cap Stocks**: Companies with a relatively small market capitalization. They may have higher growth potential but also carry higher risk.

- **Mid-Cap Stocks**: Companies with a market capitalization between small-cap and large-cap. They offer a balance of growth potential and stability.
- **Large-Cap Stocks**: Companies with a significant market capitalization. They are often well-established, stable, and widely recognized.

8.   Penny Stocks: Low-Priced, High-Risk Stocks

Penny stocks are low-priced stocks, often trading for less than a dollar per share. These stocks are associated with higher risk due to their volatile nature and potential for manipulation. Investors should exercise caution when trading penny stocks.

9.   Cyclical and Defensive Stocks: Market Sensitivity

Cyclical stocks belong to industries that are sensitive to economic cycles. Their performance tends to fluctuate with the overall economy. Defensive stocks, on the other hand, belong to industries that are less affected by economic downturns, such as utilities and consumer staples.

10. Growth and Income Stocks: Dual Focus

Some stocks offer a combination of growth potential and dividend income. Growth and income stocks seek to provide investors with both capital appreciation and regular dividend payments, offering a balance between risk and return.

Understanding these different types of stocks allows investors to diversify their portfolios effectively and align their investment choices with their financial objectives and risk tolerance. A well-balanced portfolio may include a mix of growth, value, dividends, and other stocks to capture various market opportunities and manage risk.

1.4 Key Market Players

The functioning of financial markets, including the stock market, involves a diverse array of participants, each playing a crucial role in shaping market dynamics, liquidity, and investor confidence. These key market players contribute to the overall efficiency and vitality of the market. Here's a comprehensive overview of the various key market players in the stock market:

1. Investors: Foundation of Market Demand

Investors form the bedrock of the stock market, comprising individuals, institutions, and organizations that buy and sell stocks. They include retail investors seeking personal financial goals and institutional investors such as mutual funds, pension funds, and hedge funds that manage funds on behalf of clients. Investors' buying and selling activities determine stock prices and drive market trends.

2. Traders: Facilitating Transactions

Traders are individuals or firms that actively engage in buying and selling stocks for short-term gains. They aim to capitalize on price fluctuations and market inefficiencies. Traders use technical and fundamental analysis, algorithmic trading, and other strategies to make informed trading decisions.

3. Brokers: Intermediaries in Trading

Brokers act as intermediaries between buyers and sellers. They facilitate the execution of trades on stock exchanges or other trading platforms. Online brokerage platforms have enabled individuals to access the stock market directly, while full-service brokers offer personalized advice and assistance.

4. Stock Exchanges: Market Infrastructure

Stock exchanges, such as the New York Stock Exchange (NYSE) and NASDAQ, provide the infrastructure for buying and selling stocks. They offer a centralized marketplace where buyers and sellers interact, ensuring transparency, fairness, and regulatory compliance in the trading process.

5. Market Makers: Ensuring Liquidity

Market makers are specialized entities that facilitate trading by ensuring there is a ready supply of stocks available for purchase or sale. They maintain a bid and ask price for specific stocks, contributing to market liquidity. Market makers profit from the bid-ask spread.

6. Institutional Investors: Market Shapers

Institutional investors, including mutual funds, pension funds, and insurance companies, manage large pools of capital on behalf of clients or beneficiaries. Their size and influence make them significant market players, as their investment decisions can impact stock prices and market trends.

7. Regulators: Upholding Market Integrity

Regulatory bodies, such as the U.S. Securities and Exchange Commission (SEC), oversee and regulate the stock market. They ensure that market participants adhere to rules and regulations, preventing fraud, market manipulation, and other unethical practices.

8. Financial Analysts: Providing Insights

Financial analysts study companies, industries, and economic trends to provide insights and recommendations to investors. Their research helps investors make informed decisions about buying or selling stocks. Analysts may work for investment banks, research firms, or financial news outlets.

9. Media and Financial News Outlets: Information Dissemination

Media outlets play a vital role in disseminating information about stock market developments, economic indicators, and corporate news.

Investors rely on financial news to stay informed about market trends and events that may impact their investment decisions.

10. Central Banks: Economic Influencers

Central banks, such as the Federal Reserve in the United States, influence the stock market indirectly through monetary policy. Decisions regarding interest rates and money supply can impact investor sentiment, borrowing costs, and overall market conditions.

11. Company Executives: Corporate Leadership

Company executives, including CEOs and CFOs, play a role in shaping investor perceptions through earnings reports, financial disclosures, and strategic decisions. Their leadership impacts a company's stock performance and market reputation.

12. Market Data Providers: Information Services

Market data providers offer real-time stock prices, charts, and financial news to investors and traders. These services enable market participants to access crucial information for making investment decisions.

Understanding the roles and interactions of these key market players is essential for comprehending the dynamics of the stock market. Each player contributes to the market's vibrancy, liquidity, and efficiency, collectively shaping the landscape in which investors make decisions and companies raise capital.

Chapter 1: Building a Strong Knowledge Foundation

In the ever-evolving landscape of finance, building a strong knowledge foundation is not just a desirable trait; it's a fundamental requirement for making informed decisions, minimizing risks, and achieving financial goals. Whether you're a novice embarking on your investment journey or a seasoned investor looking to refine your strategies, a robust understanding of financial concepts and principles is the bedrock upon which success is built. This comprehensive guide delves into the essential components of building a strong knowledge foundation in the world of finance, spanning from fundamental concepts to advanced strategies.

1. Understanding the Basics of Finance: Laying the Groundwork

A solid knowledge foundation begins with understanding the basic concepts of finance:

a. **Time Value of Money**: Appreciating the concept that money's value changes over time due to factors like inflation and interest rates.

b. **Risk and Return**: Grasping the relationship between risk and potential return and learning to manage risk through diversification and asset allocation.

c. **Compound Interest**: Recognizing the power of compound interest in growing investments over time and the benefits of starting early.

d. **Financial Instruments**: Familiarizing yourself with various financial instruments such as stocks, bonds, mutual funds, and exchange-traded funds (ETFs).

e. **Budgeting and Savings**: Learning to create a budget, manage expenses, and cultivate a disciplined savings habit.

2. Building a Strong Foundation in Investment Basics:

Understanding investment fundamentals is crucial for making informed decisions:

a. **Stocks and Bonds**: Delving into the mechanics of stocks as ownership shares and bonds as debt instruments.
b. **Investment Risks**: Identifying and evaluating different types of investment risks, including market, credit, liquidity, and geopolitical risks.
c. **Asset Allocation**: Grasping the concept of diversifying investments across different asset classes (stocks, bonds, real estate, etc.) to manage risk.
d. **Investment Goals and Time Horizon**: Defining clear investment goals and determining your time horizon to align your investment strategy.
e. **Investment Strategies**: Exploring various investment strategies, such as value investing, growth investing, and income investing.

3. Mastering Stock Market Concepts:

A deeper understanding of the stock market lays the groundwork for successful investing:

a. **Stock Market Mechanics**: Learning how stock exchanges function, how stocks are traded, and the role of market indices.
b. **Market Trends**: Recognizing the difference between bull and bear markets and understanding their impact on investment strategies.
c. **Fundamental vs. Technical Analysis**: Distinguishing between fundamental analysis (evaluating a company's financials) and technical analysis (studying price patterns) to make informed investment decisions.
d. **Market Order Types**: Understanding the differences between market orders, limit orders, and stop-loss orders in executing trades.
e. **Economic Indicators**: Exploring key economic indicators like GDP, unemployment rates, and inflation, and understanding how they impact stock markets.

4. Embracing Advanced Financial Concepts:

For those seeking a deeper level of expertise, advanced financial concepts offer valuable insights:

a. **Options and Futures**: Understanding derivatives like options and futures, which allow investors to speculate on price movements and manage risk.
b. **Portfolio Management**: Mastering the art of constructing and managing investment portfolios to achieve diversification and optimal risk-return balance.
c. **Behavioral Finance**: Exploring how psychological biases influence investment decisions and learning to make rational choices.

d. **Tax Efficiency**: Exploring strategies to minimize taxes on investment gains, such as tax-efficient investing and retirement accounts.
e. **Global Markets**: Gaining insights into international investing, exchange rates, and the impacts of geopolitical events on financial markets.

5. Continuous Learning and Resources:

In the dynamic world of finance, continuous learning is essential:

a. **Books and Educational Material**: Accessing reputable books, articles, and educational resources on finance and investing.
b. **Online Courses**: Enrolling in online courses or workshops that cover a wide range of financial topics.
c. **Financial News and Media**: Staying informed through financial news outlets, podcasts, and video content.
d. **Financial Advisors**: Seeking guidance from certified financial advisors to navigate complex financial situations and tailor strategies to individual goals.
e. **Investment Simulators**: Using investment simulators or virtual trading platforms to practice investment strategies without real money.

In conclusion, building a strong knowledge foundation in finance is a journey that encompasses fundamental concepts, investment strategies, market dynamics, and advanced financial principles. Whether you're aiming for personal financial security, wealth accumulation, or the pursuit of investment success, an educated approach is the key. By delving into the basics, mastering investment essentials, and continuously expanding your knowledge, you empower yourself to navigate the complexities of the financial world with confidence and make well-informed decisions that align with your goals. Remember, in the realm of finance, knowledge truly is the currency of success.

2.1 Stock Market Terminology

Stepping into the realm of stock trading and investment can be both exciting and daunting, especially when faced with a barrage of unfamiliar terms and jargon. Developing a solid grasp of stock market terminology is akin to acquiring a new language – one that empowers you to communicate effectively in the financial world, make informed decisions, and navigate the complexities of the market with confidence. This comprehensive guide delves into key stock market terms, unraveling their meanings and significance to help you build a strong foundation for success.

1. **Stock and Ownership:**

-   **Stock**: At the heart of the stock market lies the concept of a "stock." A stock, also known as a share or equity, represents ownership in a company. When you own a stock, you hold a fractional ownership stake in that company, granting you certain rights and potential benefits.
-   **Dividend**: Companies often distribute a portion of their earnings to shareholders as dividends. These are cash payments made regularly or occasionally, offering investors a source of passive income.

- **IPO (Initial Public Offering)**: When a private company goes public, it offers its shares for sale to the general public for the first time. This process is known as an IPO, and it marks a significant event in the company's journey.
- **Market Capitalization**: The market capitalization of a company is the total value of all its outstanding shares. It's calculated by multiplying the stock price by the number of shares. Market capitalization categorizes companies into different size segments, such as large-cap, mid-cap, and small-cap.
- **Market Order**: A market order is an instruction to buy or sell a stock at the current market price. It's executed quickly, but the actual price may slightly differ due to market fluctuations.
- **Limit Order**: A limit order is a specific instruction to buy or sell a stock at a designated price or better. It ensures a certain price but may not guarantee immediate execution.

2. **Investment Strategies:**

Value Investing: Value investors seek stocks that they believe are trading below their intrinsic value. They analyze a company's financials and fundamentals to identify potential bargains.

- **Growth Investing**: Growth investors focus on companies that are expected to experience rapid earnings growth. These companies often reinvest their profits to fuel expansion and innovation.
- **Income Investing**: Income investors prioritize stocks that offer regular dividend payments. They seek stability and consistent income streams, often investing in well-established companies.

- **Diversification**: Diversification involves spreading investments across various asset classes, sectors, and industries to reduce risk. It's a strategy to avoid putting all your eggs in one basket.
- **Portfolio**: A portfolio is a collection of investments held by an individual or entity. It's a mix of stocks, bonds, and other assets tailored to meet specific financial goals.

3. **Market Trends and Conditions:**

- **Bull Market**: A bull market is characterized by rising stock prices and overall optimism. Investors are confident in the market's upward trajectory.
- **Bear Market**: A bear market is marked by falling stock prices and pessimism. It's a period of market decline that lasts at least 20% from recent highs.
- **Correction**: A correction is a short-term decline in stock prices, usually around 10%, after a sustained period of gains.
- **Volatility**: Volatility refers to the rapid and unpredictable price changes of a stock or the market. It's a measure of the fluctuations in price over time.

4. **Technical Analysis:**

- **Technical Analysis**: Technical analysis involves studying stock price charts, patterns, and trading volume to predict future price movements. It's based on the belief that historical price trends can forecast future performance.

- **Support and Resistance**: Support is a price level at which a stock often stops falling, while resistance is a level where it tends to stop rising. These levels are essential in analyzing price trends.
- **Moving Average**: A moving average is an average of a stock's prices over a specific period. It smooths out short-term fluctuations, aiding in identifying trends.
- **RSI (Relative Strength Index)**: The RSI is a momentum oscillator that measures the speed and change of price movements. It helps identify overbought or oversold conditions.
- **MACD (Moving Average Convergence Divergence)**: The MACD is a trend-following indicator that shows the relationship between two moving averages. It assists in identifying potential trend changes.

5. **Fundamental Analysis:**

Fundamental Analysis: Fundamental analysis involves evaluating a company's financial health, earnings, management quality, and industry position. It's about understanding the company behind the stock.

- **EPS (Earnings Per Share)**: EPS is a company's net earnings divided by the number of outstanding shares. It's a key measure of profitability.
- **P/E Ratio (Price-to-Earnings Ratio)**: The P/E ratio is the ratio of a company's stock price to its earnings per share. It's a valuation metric indicating how much investors are willing to pay for each dollar of earnings.

- **ROE (Return on Equity)**: ROE is a measure of a company's profitability relative to shareholders' equity. It indicates how efficiently a company generates profits from its equity.
- **Debt-to-Equity Ratio**: The debt-to-equity ratio compares a company's debt to its equity. It measures financial leverage and risk.

6. **Economic Indicators:**

- **GDP (Gross Domestic Product)**: GDP measures the total value of goods and services produced within a country. It's a critical indicator of economic health.
- **Inflation**: Inflation is the rate at which the general price level of goods and services rises, eroding purchasing power.
- **Unemployment Rate**: The unemployment rate indicates the percentage of the labor force that is jobless and actively seeking employment.
- **Consumer Confidence**: Consumer confidence measures public sentiment about the overall state of the economy. It influences spending patterns.

7. **Risk and Risk Management:**

- **Risk**: Risk refers to the possibility of loss or failure. In investing, risk is inherent, and understanding and managing it is crucial.
- **Diversifiable Risk**: Diversifiable risk, also known as unsystematic risk, can be reduced through diversification. It's specific to a company or industry.

- **Systematic Risk**: Systematic risk, also known as market risk, affects the entire market and cannot be eliminated through diversification.
- **Stop-Loss Order**: A stop-loss order is a predetermined point at which an investor will sell a stock to limit potential losses.

8. Investor Psychology:

- **Herd Mentality**: Herd mentality is the tendency of individuals to follow the actions of a larger group. It can lead to irrational decision-making.
- **Confirmation Bias**: Confirmation bias is the inclination to favor information that confirms existing beliefs while disregarding contradictory data.

9. Long-Term Perspective:

- **Buy and Hold**: Buy and hold is a long-term investment strategy where investors purchase stocks with the intention of holding onto them for an extended period.
- **Compound Interest**: Compound interest is the interest earned not only on the initial investment but also on the accumulated interest over time.

10. Market Indices:

- **Dow Jones Industrial Average (DJIA)**: The DJIA is an index that tracks the performance of 30 large, publicly traded companies in the United States.
- **S&P 500**: The S&P 500 is an index of 500 leading companies across various industries, considered a benchmark for the U.S. stock market.
- **NASDAQ Composite**: The NASDAQ Composite is an index of all common stocks listed on the NASDAQ stock exchange.

11. Financial News and Media:

- **Bullish**: Being bullish signifies a positive outlook on stock prices or the overall market.
- **Bearish**: Being bearish signifies a negative outlook on stock prices or the market's direction.
- **Market Sentiment**: Market sentiment refers to the overall attitude of investors toward the market's future direction.

12. Market Manipulation:

- **Pump and Dump**: Pump and dump is a fraudulent practice where a stock's price is artificially inflated (pumped) and then sold off (dumped) for profit.
- **Insider Trading**: Insider trading involves trading a company's securities based on non-public information, which is illegal and unethical.

13. Central Bank Influence:

- Federal Reserve (Fed): The Federal Reserve, or the Fed, is the central bank of the United States. It plays a crucial role in monetary policy and setting interest rates.

14. Analyst Recommendations:

- Buy, Hold, Sell: Analyst recommendations indicate whether a stock is recommended for buying, holding, or selling.

15. Short Selling:

- Short Selling: Short selling involves borrowing shares and selling them with the expectation that their price will decrease. The goal is to buy them back at a lower price and return them to the lender.

16. Options and Derivatives:

- **Call Option**: A call option grants the holder the right but not the obligation to buy a stock at a predetermined price before a specified expiration date.
- **Put Option**: A put option grants the holder the right but not the obligation to sell a stock at a predetermined price before a specified expiration date.

17. Corporate Actions:

- **Dividend Yield**: The dividend yield is the annual dividend income relative to the stock's price. It's expressed as a percentage.
- **Stock Split**: A stock split involves dividing existing shares into multiple shares. Although the number of shares increases, the total value remains unchanged.

18. Technical Indicators:

- Moving Average Convergence Divergence (MACD): MACD is a trend-following indicator that helps identify changes in the strength, direction, momentum, and duration of a trend.

In conclusion, venturing into the world of stock trading and investing requires fluency in its unique terminology. This guide has demystified essential stock market terms, empowering you with the knowledge needed to communicate effectively in the financial landscape. Armed with these insights, you're better equipped to make informed decisions, adapt to market dynamics, and pursue your financial goals with confidence.

2.2 Economic Indicators and Their Impact

Economic indicators are vital tools that provide insights into the health and direction of an economy. They offer valuable data points that help economists, policymakers, investors, and analysts assess the overall economic performance, make informed decisions, and predict future trends. These indicators have a profound impact on financial markets, influencing investment strategies, market sentiment, and trading activities. This guide explores key economic indicators and their significant influence on the financial landscape.

1. GDP (Gross Domestic Product):

GDP is arguably the most critical economic indicator, measuring the total value of all goods and services produced within a country's borders. It serves as a barometer of an economy's size and growth. Investors closely monitor GDP reports, as they provide insights into economic expansion or contraction. When GDP grows, it signals a healthy economy, boosting investor confidence and potentially leading to stock market gains. Conversely, a decline in GDP can prompt concerns about economic downturns and lead to market volatility.

2. Inflation Rate:

Inflation, the rate at which the general price level of goods and services rises, is a crucial indicator of purchasing power and economic stability. Central banks, like the Federal Reserve, use inflation targets to guide their monetary policy decisions. Moderate inflation is generally seen as healthy for economic growth, as it encourages consumer spending. However, high or rapidly rising inflation can erode purchasing power and create uncertainty. In response to rising inflation, central banks may raise interest rates to cool down economic activity and stabilize prices. Such actions can impact bond yields, borrowing costs, and stock market performance.

3. Unemployment Rate:

The unemployment rate reflects the percentage of the labor force that is jobless and actively seeking employment. A low unemployment rate is indicative of a strong economy and consumer spending. When people are employed, they have income to spend on goods and services, contributing to economic growth. Conversely, high unemployment rates can lead to reduced consumer spending and economic slowdowns. The impact on financial markets is significant, with lower unemployment rates contributing to positive investor sentiment and potential stock market gains.

4. Interest Rates:

Interest rates set by central banks influence borrowing costs, consumer spending, and investment decisions. When interest rates are low, borrowing becomes cheaper, stimulating economic activity and boosting stock markets. Conversely, higher interest rates can discourage borrowing and spending, potentially leading to decreased corporate earnings and slower economic growth. Investors closely monitor central bank meetings for hints about potential changes in interest rates, as rate adjustments can have a profound impact on stock, bond, and currency markets.

5. Consumer Confidence Index:

The Consumer Confidence Index gauges consumers' sentiment about their economic prospects. High consumer confidence typically translates to increased spending and economic growth. Positive consumer sentiment can contribute to higher demand for goods and services, driving corporate profits and potentially benefiting stock markets. Conversely, low consumer confidence can lead to reduced spending, potentially dampening economic activity and causing market uncertainty.

6. Purchasing Managers' Index (PMI):

The PMI is an indicator of manufacturing and services sector health. It assesses factors like new orders, production, employment, and supplier deliveries. A PMI reading above 50 indicates expansion, while a reading below 50 suggests contraction. A strong PMI can lead to positive investor sentiment, as it indicates economic growth and potential stock market gains. Conversely, a weak PMI may lead to concerns about economic slowdown and market volatility.

7. Retail Sales:

Retail sales data provides insights into consumer spending patterns. Strong retail sales figures suggest robust consumer demand, driving economic growth and boosting stock markets. However, weak retail sales may raise concerns about an economic slowdown and negatively impact market sentiment.

8. Housing Market Indicators:

Indicators like housing starts, building permits, and home sales reflect the health of the real estate sector. A strong housing market is often associated with economic growth and positive market sentiment. Rising home sales and construction activity can lead to increased consumer spending and investments, benefiting stock markets. Conversely, a downturn in the housing market can trigger economic concerns and market volatility.

In conclusion, economic indicators play a pivotal role in shaping financial markets. Investors, policymakers, and analysts use these indicators to gauge economic health, predict trends, and make informed decisions. The impact of economic indicators on financial markets is far-reaching, influencing investment strategies, market sentiment, and trading activities. Being attuned to these indicators enables market participants to navigate the dynamic financial landscape with greater clarity and confidence.

2.3 Analyzing Company Financials

Analyzing a company's financials is a critical skill for investors, analysts, and stakeholders seeking to make informed decisions about their investments. By delving into a company's financial statements, one can gain valuable insights into its performance, stability, and growth prospects. This guide provides a comprehensive overview of how to analyze company financials and interpret key financial statements.

1. **Financial Statements Overview:**

Financial statements are essential documents that provide a snapshot of a company's financial health. The three primary financial statements are:

a. **Income Statement**: Also known as the profit and loss statement (P&L), it outlines a company's revenues, expenses, and net income over a specific period. This statement reveals the company's profitability and operational efficiency.

b. **Balance Sheet**: The balance sheet provides a snapshot of a company's financial position at a given point in time. It shows assets, liabilities, and shareholders' equity, illustrating the company's financial structure and solvency.

c. **Cash Flow Statement**: This statement details the inflows and outflows of cash during a specific period. It highlights a company's ability to generate and manage cash, a crucial aspect of its operations.

2. **Key Financial Ratios:**

Financial ratios provide valuable insights into various aspects of a company's performance. Here are some key ratios to consider:

a. **Liquidity Ratios**: These ratios assess a company's ability to meet short-term obligations.

- Current Ratio: Current assets divided by current liabilities.
- Quick Ratio (Acid-Test Ratio): (Current Assets - Inventory) divided by current liabilities.

b. **Solvency Ratios**: These ratios measure a company's long-term financial stability.

- Debt-to-Equity Ratio: Total debt divided by shareholders' equity.
- Interest Coverage Ratio: Earnings before interest and taxes (EBIT) divided by interest expense.

c. **Profitability Ratios**: These ratios evaluate a company's ability to generate profits.

- Gross Profit Margin: (Gross Profit / Revenue) multiplied by 100.
- Net Profit Margin: (Net Income / Revenue) multiplied by 100.
- Return on Assets (ROA): Net income divided by total assets.
- Return on Equity (ROE): Net income divided by shareholders' equity.

d. **Efficiency Ratios**: These ratios assess how effectively a company utilizes its resources.

- Asset Turnover Ratio: Revenue divided by total assets.
- Inventory Turnover Ratio: Cost of goods sold divided by average inventory.

e. **Market Ratios**: These ratios relate a company's stock price to its financial performance.

- Price-to-Earnings Ratio (P/E): Stock price divided by earnings per share.
- Price-to-Sales Ratio (P/S): Stock price divided by revenue per share.

- Price-to-Book Ratio (P/B): Stock price divided by book value per share.

3. Trend Analysis:

Comparing a company's financial data over multiple periods is crucial for identifying trends and patterns. Trend analysis helps assess whether a company's financial performance is improving, declining, or remaining stable over time.

4. Vertical and Horizontal Analysis:

Vertical analysis involves expressing each line item on the financial statements as a percentage of a base item. Horizontal analysis, on the other hand, compares line items across different periods to highlight changes in values and percentages.

5. Common-Size Financial Statements:

Common-size financial statements express all line items as a percentage of total revenue. This allows for easy comparison of the relative proportions of different components.

6. Qualitative Factors:

In addition to quantitative analysis, it's important to consider qualitative factors that can impact a company's financial performance. These factors may include industry trends, competitive positioning, management quality, regulatory environment, and market sentiment.

7. Comparisons and Benchmarks:

Comparing a company's financial ratios and performance to those of its peers and industry benchmarks provides context and helps identify strengths and weaknesses.

8. DuPont Analysis:

DuPont analysis breaks down a company's return on equity (ROE) into its components: profitability, asset turnover, and financial leverage. This analysis provides insights into the drivers of a company's ROE.

9. Cash Flow Analysis:

Analyzing the cash flow statement helps assess a company's ability to generate cash and manage its operating, investing, and financing activities.

10. Sensitivity and Scenario Analysis:

Incorporate sensitivity and scenario analysis to understand how changes in key variables, such as revenue, costs, and interest rates, could impact a company's financials and overall performance.

11. Limitations and Qualifications:

It's important to recognize the limitations of financial analysis, including potential accounting biases, industry-specific considerations, and the impact of external factors beyond financial statements.

In conclusion, analyzing company financials is a multidimensional process that combines quantitative metrics, trend analysis, and qualitative considerations. It enables investors and analysts to gain a comprehensive understanding of a company's financial performance, strengths, weaknesses, and growth potential. A robust financial analysis forms the basis for informed investment decisions, strategic planning, and risk assessment in the dynamic world of business and finance.

2.4 Research Tools and Resources

In the fast-paced and information-rich landscape of finance and investing, having access to reliable research tools and resources is essential for making well-informed decisions. Whether you're a seasoned investor, a trader, or someone just starting to explore the world of finance, having the right tools at your disposal can significantly enhance your ability to analyze markets, evaluate investments, and stay updated on the latest developments. This guide outlines a range of research tools and resources that can empower you to navigate the complexities of the financial world with confidence.

1. **Financial News and Analysis Platforms:**

- Bloomberg: A comprehensive platform offering real-time financial news, data, and analysis on global markets, companies, and economic trends.
- Reuters: A trusted source of breaking news, financial information, and analysis spanning various industries and regions.
- CNBC: A popular financial news channel and website providing market coverage, expert insights, and interviews with industry professionals.

2. **Financial Data and Research Providers:**

- Morningstar: Offers detailed research, analysis, and ratings on stocks, mutual funds, exchange-traded funds (ETFs), and more.
- FactSet: Provides financial data, analytics, and tools for investment professionals, including portfolio analysis and market intelligence.
- Thomson Reuters Eikon: A platform offering financial information, data visualization tools, and real-time market insights.

3. **Stock Market Analysis and Screening Tools:**

- Finviz: A stock market visualization platform that provides stock screening, technical analysis, and heat maps.
- StockCharts: Offers customizable charts, technical analysis tools, and scanning capabilities for various markets.
- Zacks Investment Research: Provides stock research, analysis, and ranking tools to help investors identify potential opportunities.

4. Fundamental and Technical Analysis Platforms:

- Yahoo Finance: Offers a wealth of financial information, including stock quotes, news, historical data, and basic charts.
- Investopedia: Features educational content on investing, trading strategies, and financial concepts, along with market news and analysis.
- Seeking Alpha: A platform for crowdsourced investment research, featuring articles, analysis, and discussions by investors and experts.

5. Economic and Market Data Providers:

- Federal Reserve Economic Data (FRED): Provides a vast collection of economic data, indicators, and charts maintained by the Federal Reserve Bank of St. Louis.
- Trading Economics: Offers a wide range of economic indicators, historical data, and forecasts for various countries.
- World Bank Data: Provides global economic, social, and environmental data for in-depth analysis and research.

6. Corporate Filings and Financial Statements:

- U.S. Securities and Exchange Commission (SEC): Offers access to company filings, financial statements, and other important documents through its EDGAR database.

- Corporate Websites: Many publicly traded companies provide their financial reports, investor presentations, and other relevant information on their official websites.

7. Research Reports and Analyst Recommendations:

- Research Firms: Institutions like Goldman Sachs, J.P. Morgan, and Morgan Stanley publish research reports and analyst recommendations on various stocks and sectors.
- Brokerage Platforms: Online brokerage platforms often provide research reports, ratings, and insights for their clients.

8. Social Media and Online Communities:

- Twitter: Follow financial news outlets, analysts, and industry experts for real-time updates and insights.
- Reddit: Subreddits like r/investing and r/stocks offer discussions, opinions, and insights from a wide range of investors.

9. Educational Resources:

- Coursera, Udemy, Khan Academy: Online platforms offering courses on finance, investing, trading, and economics.
- Investment Books: There's a plethora of books written by renowned investors and experts, covering various aspects of finance and investing.

10. Professional Organizations and Forums:

- CFA Institute: Offers resources, research, and networking opportunities for professionals in the investment management industry.
- Financial Forums: Platforms like Wall Street Oasis and Bogleheads provide forums for discussions and insights from finance professionals and enthusiasts.

In conclusion, the financial landscape offers a wealth of research tools and resources to help individuals stay informed, analyze markets, and make sound investment decisions. Whether you're looking for real-time market data, economic indicators, company information, or educational content, these tools can serve as valuable companions on your journey to financial understanding and success. Remember that staying curious, continuously learning, and critically evaluating information is key to effectively utilizing these resources for your benefit.

Chapter 3: Developing Profitable Trading Strategies

Creating profitable trading strategies is both an art and a science, requiring a blend of research, analysis, discipline, and adaptability. While there's no one-size-fits-all approach, successful traders follow a systematic process to formulate strategies that align with their goals, risk tolerance, and market conditions. This guide offers a comprehensive framework for developing profitable trading strategies that can potentially yield consistent returns.

1. Define Your Trading Goals:

Before crafting a strategy, clarify your objectives. Are you aiming for short-term gains, long-term growth, or a balance of both? Understand your risk tolerance, time horizon, and financial goals to shape your strategy accordingly.

2. Choose a Trading Style:

Different trading styles suit different personalities and risk profiles. Common styles include:

- Day Trading: Buying and selling within the same trading day to capitalize on short-term price movements.
- Swing Trading: Holding positions for a few days to weeks, seeking to capture price swings.

- Position Trading: Holding positions for weeks to months, based on longer-term trends and fundamentals.

3. Conduct Market Analysis:

Understand the market you're trading in. Perform fundamental and technical analysis to identify trends, patterns, and potential opportunities. Consider macroeconomic factors, industry news, and market sentiment.

4. Select Your Assets:

Choose the financial instruments you'll trade, such as stocks, forex, commodities, or cryptocurrencies. Focus on markets you understand and can monitor effectively.

5. Develop Entry and Exit Rules:

Establish clear criteria for entering and exiting trades. This could include specific technical indicators, price levels, or news triggers. Define stop-loss and take-profit levels to manage risk and secure profits.

6. Risk Management:

Protecting your capital is paramount. Determine how much of your capital you're willing to risk on each trade (risk per trade). Common risk management rules include risking 1-2% of your capital on a single trade.

7. Backtesting:

Test your strategy's performance using historical data. Backtesting helps you assess how your strategy would have performed in the past, providing insights into its potential strengths and weaknesses.

8. Paper Trading:

Before committing real money, practice your strategy in a simulated environment. This helps you refine your approach, gain confidence, and identify any adjustments needed.

9. Real-Time Testing:

Implement your strategy with a small amount of capital initially. Monitor its performance in real-time and make necessary refinements based on actual market conditions.

10. Monitor and Adapt:

Markets evolve, and strategies need to adapt. Continuously monitor your strategy's performance, and be prepared to tweak it in response to changing market dynamics.

11. Psychological Discipline:

Trading psychology plays a vital role. Emotions can lead to impulsive decisions. Stick to your strategy, manage emotions, and avoid chasing losses.

12. Continuous Learning:

Stay updated with market trends, economic events, and new trading techniques. Learning from successes and failures helps refine your strategy over time.

13. Record Keeping:

Maintain a trading journal to document your trades, rationale, outcomes, and emotions. Reviewing your journal can reveal patterns and insights to refine your strategy further.

14. Diversification:

Avoid putting all your capital into a single trade or asset. Diversification helps mitigate risk by spreading exposure across different instruments.

15. Adaptive Strategies:

Recognize when market conditions change and adjust your strategy accordingly. What works in a trending market might not be effective in a range-bound one.

16. Continuous Evaluation:

Regularly assess your strategy's performance against your goals. If it's not yielding the desired results, be open to modifying or even discarding it.

17. Risk-Reward Ratio:

Evaluate potential profits against potential losses for each trade. A favorable risk-reward ratio helps ensure that winning trades can offset losing ones.

In conclusion, developing profitable trading strategies requires a systematic approach that encompasses market analysis, risk management, disciplined execution, and adaptability. It's essential to align your strategies with your goals, risk tolerance, and trading style, while continuously learning and adjusting based on real-world experiences. Remember that there's no one guaranteed formula for success, but by following a structured approach and staying disciplined, you can increase your chances of developing strategies that stand the test of time and market fluctuations.

3.1 Fundamental Analysis

Fundamental analysis stands as one of the cornerstone methodologies in the world of investing. Rooted in the belief that the true value of a financial asset is derived from its intrinsic attributes, this approach delves deep into a company's financials, management, industry trends, and economic factors to assess its worth. Whether you're a novice investor or a seasoned market player, understanding the intricacies of fundamental analysis is essential for making informed investment decisions. This comprehensive guide explores the key components, methods, and benefits of fundamental analysis.

Understanding Fundamental Analysis:

At its core, fundamental analysis involves a comprehensive evaluation of a company's intrinsic value, aiming to determine whether its stock is overvalued, undervalued, or fairly priced. It assumes that the market may sometimes misprice stocks, presenting opportunities for astute investors to capitalize on discrepancies between market price and a company's true worth.

Key Components of Fundamental Analysis:

1. Financial Statements:

Financial statements serve as the bedrock of fundamental analysis. These documents—comprising the income statement, balance sheet, and cash flow statement—provide insights into a company's financial health, performance, and cash flow dynamics. By analyzing revenue, expenses, assets, liabilities, and equity, investors gain a comprehensive view of a company's operations and financial stability.

2. Earnings and Profitability:

Earnings growth is a crucial indicator of a company's health. Investors examine factors like earnings per share (EPS), net income, and profit margins to gauge profitability trends. Companies with consistent and increasing earnings often attract investor confidence.

3. Valuation Ratios:

Valuation ratios compare a company's market price to its underlying financial metrics. Common ratios include:

- **Price-to-Earnings (P/E) Ratio**: Compares a company's stock price to its earnings per share, helping investors assess if a stock is under- or overvalued.
- **Price-to-Book (P/B) Ratio**: Compares a company's stock price to its book value per share, indicating whether the stock is trading above or below its intrinsic value.
- **Price-to-Sales (P/S) Ratio**: Measures a company's stock price relative to its revenue per share, providing insights into its revenue generation efficiency.

4. Dividend Analysis:

Dividend-paying companies often attract income-seeking investors. Analyzing dividend history, payout ratios, and dividend yields helps assess a company's commitment to returning value to shareholders.

5. Management Quality:

Strong and capable management is pivotal to a company's success. Evaluating management's track record, corporate governance practices, and strategic decision-making provides insights into a company's long-term viability.

6. Industry and Competitive Analysis:

Understanding a company's industry dynamics, competitive landscape, and market trends helps investors assess its position in the market. Industry growth potential and a company's ability to maintain a competitive advantage are vital considerations.

7. Economic and Macroeconomic Factors:

External factors like economic indicators, interest rates, and government policies influence a company's performance. Analyzing how macroeconomic trends impact a company's operations and revenue streams is crucial.

Methods of Fundamental Analysis:

1. Top-Down Approach:

In the top-down approach, investors start by analyzing broader economic trends and then narrow down to specific industries and companies. This method helps identify industries poised for growth, which then guides the selection of individual stocks within those sectors.

2. Bottom-Up Approach:

The bottom-up approach focuses on analyzing individual companies first, regardless of their industry or sector. Investors seek well-managed companies with strong fundamentals, aiming to build a diversified portfolio from these selections.

Benefits of Fundamental Analysis:

1. Informed Decision-Making:

Fundamental analysis equips investors with a deep understanding of a company's financial health, growth potential, and competitive position. This knowledge guides prudent investment choices aligned with long-term goals.

2. Long-Term Perspective:

Fundamental analysis is particularly valuable for long-term investors aiming to hold assets over extended periods. It helps identify companies with solid foundations and sustainable growth prospects.

3. Risk Mitigation:

By thoroughly evaluating a company's financials and industry position, investors can identify potential risks and make more informed risk-management decisions.

4. Value Investing:

Value investors seek stocks trading below their intrinsic value. Fundamental analysis allows them to uncover these undervalued gems and potentially capitalize on market mispricings.

5. Cyclical and Contrarian Plays:

Understanding a company's fundamentals can lead to opportunities in cyclical industries or contrarian plays, where temporary downturns may create buying opportunities for patient investors.

Limitations and Challenges:

Fundamental analysis isn't without its limitations. Factors like market sentiment, unpredictable events, and irrational investor behavior can impact stock prices despite strong fundamentals. Moreover, conducting thorough analysis requires time, effort, and expertise, which may deter some investors.

Fundamental analysis serves as a potent tool for investors seeking to make informed decisions based on a company's intrinsic value, financial performance, and growth potential. It offers a systematic approach to understanding the dynamics of the business world, empowering investors to navigate the complexities of the financial markets with greater confidence. By blending financial statements, industry insights, economic trends, and valuation metrics, investors can develop a holistic perspective that guides their investment choices toward achieving their financial objectives.

3.2 Technical Analysis

Technical analysis is a method used by traders and investors to evaluate financial markets and forecast price movements by analyzing historical price data and trading volumes. Unlike fundamental analysis, which focuses on a company's financials and intrinsic value, technical analysis relies on charts, patterns, and indicators to identify trends and potential trading opportunities. This guide provides an in-depth exploration of technical analysis, its key principles, tools, and its application in the dynamic world of trading.

Understanding Technical Analysis:

Technical analysis operates under the premise that historical price movements contain valuable information about future price movements. By studying patterns, trends, and indicators, practitioners attempt to predict the future direction of prices, aiming to profit from these anticipated moves.

Key Principles of Technical Analysis:

1. Market Discounts Everything:

Technical analysis assumes that all available information, whether public or private, is already reflected in a security's price. This includes news, earnings reports, and macroeconomic data.

2. Price Moves in Trends:

Price movements tend to follow trends—uptrends, downtrends, or sideways trends. Identifying and riding these trends is a fundamental principle of technical analysis.

3. History Tends to Repeat Itself:

Patterns and behaviors that occurred in the past are likely to repeat in the future. Analysts use historical price patterns to anticipate potential future movements.

4. Technicals Are More Important in Shorter Time Frames:

While fundamental analysis might be more relevant for long-term investors, technical analysis is often more effective in shorter time frames, such as day trading or swing trading.

Key Components of Technical Analysis:

1. Charts:

Charts are the backbone of technical analysis. Common types of charts include line charts, bar charts, and candlestick charts. Candlestick charts are particularly popular due to their visual representation of price movements, showing open, high, low, and closing prices.

2. Patterns:

Patterns emerge in price charts and can provide insights into potential future movements. Common patterns include:

- Trendlines: Diagonal lines drawn on charts to connect highs or lows, helping identify trends.

- Support and Resistance: Levels where a stock tends to stop falling (support) or rising (resistance).
- Head and Shoulders: A reversal pattern with three peaks resembling a head between two shoulders.

3. Indicators:

Indicators are mathematical calculations applied to price data or trading volumes, aiding in decision-making. Some popular indicators include:

- Moving Averages: Smoothed lines that help identify trends by smoothing out price fluctuations.
- Relative Strength Index (RSI): Measures the speed and change of price movements to identify overbought or oversold conditions.
- Moving Average Convergence Divergence (MACD): Measures the relationship between two moving averages to identify momentum changes.

4. Volume Analysis:

The trading volume provides insights into market participation. Higher volume during price moves can confirm trends, while lower volume might indicate reversals.

5. Chart Patterns:

Chart patterns are formations that repeat over time and signal potential price movements. Examples include:

- Double Tops and Bottoms: Patterns indicating potential trend reversals.
- Flags and Pennants: Patterns indicating continuation of existing trends.

Methods of Technical Analysis:

1. Trend Following:

Trend-following strategies involve identifying and trading in the direction of the prevailing trend. This approach aims to capitalize on extended price movements and momentum.

2. Counter-Trend Trading:

Counter-trend strategies seek to identify potential reversals in the current trend. These traders aim to profit from short-term price corrections.

3. Breakout Trading:

Breakout traders look for price movements beyond established support or resistance levels. Breakouts can signal potential strong trends.

4. Swing Trading:

Swing traders hold positions for several days to weeks, aiming to capture short- to medium-term price swings.

Benefits of Technical Analysis:

1. Timing and Entry Points:

Technical analysis can help identify optimal entry and exit points for trades, allowing traders to potentially capitalize on short-term price movements.

2. Objective Approach:

Technical analysis relies on data-driven metrics, providing a more objective approach to decision-making compared to purely emotional decisions.

3. Short-Term Trading Opportunities:

Traders who prefer short-term trading can benefit from technical analysis' ability to identify short-lived price trends and patterns.

4. Widely Applicable:

Technical analysis can be applied to various financial instruments, including stocks, forex, commodities, and cryptocurrencies.

Limitations and Challenges:

1. Subjectivity:

Interpreting charts and patterns can be subjective. Different analysts might draw different conclusions from the same data.

2. Historical Data Limitation:

Technical analysis relies on historical data, which might not always accurately predict future price movements, especially during unexpected events.

3. Self-Fulfilling Prophecy:

The popularity of certain technical patterns can lead to self-fulfilling prophecies. Traders acting on these patterns might influence price movements.

4. Rapid Changes:

In fast-moving markets, prices can change quickly, making it challenging to execute trades at desired levels.

Technical analysis offers traders a systematic approach to analyzing markets, identifying trends, and making informed trading decisions. By examining price charts, patterns, and indicators, practitioners aim to forecast potential price movements and seize opportunities for profit. While it's not foolproof and faces challenges, technical analysis remains a valuable tool in the toolkit of traders seeking to navigate the complexities of financial markets and capitalize on short-term price fluctuations.

3.3 Value Investing

Value investing is a timeless investment strategy that has gained prominence for its patient and methodical approach to the stock market. Spearheaded by legendary investors like Benjamin Graham and Warren Buffett, value investing revolves around the belief that stocks can be mispriced by the market, presenting opportunities for savvy investors to purchase them at a discount to their intrinsic value. This comprehensive guide delves into the principles, methods, advantages, and challenges of value investing, shedding light on its enduring appeal in the world of finance.

Understanding Value Investing:

At its core, value investing is centered on the principle of buying stocks that are trading below their intrinsic or fair value. This approach is in stark contrast to momentum or growth investing, where investors seek stocks with strong upward price trends and potential for rapid earnings growth. Value investors are more concerned with identifying fundamentally strong companies whose stock prices do not reflect their true worth.

Key Principles of Value Investing:

1. Intrinsic Value:

The cornerstone of value investing is the concept of intrinsic value—the true worth of a company based on its fundamental attributes. Value investors aim to purchase stocks when their market prices are below this intrinsic value, allowing them to potentially profit as the market corrects itself.

2. Margin of Safety:

Benjamin Graham, considered the father of value investing, introduced the idea of a "margin of safety." This entails buying stocks at a significant discount to their intrinsic value, providing a buffer against potential price declines or unfavorable market conditions.

3. Contrarian Thinking:

Value investors often diverge from market sentiment. They are willing to invest in companies that are temporarily out of favor or facing challenges, believing that market overreaction can create buying opportunities.

4. Long-Term Perspective:

Value investing requires patience. Investors holding undervalued stocks may need to wait for the market to recognize their worth, potentially leading to gains over the long term.

Methods of Value Investing:

1. Fundamental Analysis:

Fundamental analysis is the bedrock of value investing. Investors examine a company's financial statements, earnings, growth potential, and industry dynamics to assess its intrinsic value.

2. Price-to-Earnings (P/E) Ratio:

The P/E ratio compares a company's stock price to its earnings per share. A lower P/E ratio might indicate an undervalued stock.

3. Price-to-Book (P/B) Ratio:

The P/B ratio compares a company's stock price to its book value per share. A lower P/B ratio suggests the stock might be trading below its asset value.

4. Dividend Yield:

Companies with stable dividends can be attractive to value investors seeking income. The dividend yield compares a company's annual dividends to its stock price.

5. Earnings Yield:

The earnings yield is the inverse of the P/E ratio. It compares a company's earnings to its stock price, indicating the potential return an investor might earn on their investment.

Advantages of Value Investing:

1. Rational Decision-Making:

Value investing encourages objective analysis based on fundamental data, reducing the influence of emotions and market noise.

2. Capital Preservation:

The focus on buying undervalued stocks provides a potential cushion against market downturns.

3. Long-Term Wealth Creation:

Patient value investing can lead to significant wealth accumulation over time, especially if the market eventually recognizes the true value of the stocks.

4. Contrarian Approach:

Value investing thrives on contrarian thinking, allowing investors to capitalize on market inefficiencies.

Challenges and Considerations:

1. Time and Patience:

Value investing requires a long-term horizon, as it may take time for the market to correct and stock prices to reflect their intrinsic value.

2. Market Timing:

Identifying the right time to buy undervalued stocks can be challenging, as the market can remain irrational longer than anticipated.

3. Value Traps:

Not all stocks trading at low prices are undervalued. Some may be facing fundamental challenges that justify their lower valuations.

4. Changing Dynamics:

Market conditions, industry trends, and economic factors can impact a company's intrinsic value, requiring continuous reassessment.

Value investing embodies a disciplined and patient approach to investing that seeks to capitalize on market inefficiencies. By identifying stocks that are trading below their intrinsic value and utilizing a margin of safety, value investors aim to protect capital while positioning themselves for long-term growth. While not without its challenges, value investing remains a powerful strategy that appeals to those who appreciate rational analysis, contrarian thinking, and the potential for steady wealth creation over time. It's a testament to the enduring wisdom of legendary investors like Benjamin Graham and Warren Buffett, who have showcased the merits of seeking undervalued gems in a dynamic and ever-evolving market landscape.

3.4 Growth Investing

Growth investing is an investment strategy that revolves around identifying and investing in companies with the potential for substantial earnings growth. Unlike value investing, which focuses on undervalued stocks, growth investors seek out companies poised for expansion, innovation, and increased market share. This guide delves into the principles, methods, benefits, and challenges of growth investing, shedding light on its role in the dynamic world of finance.

Understanding Growth Investing:

Growth investing centers on identifying companies that are expected to experience above-average revenue and earnings growth compared to their industry peers. Investors are willing to pay a premium for the promise of future growth, as they anticipate that the stock price will rise in tandem with the company's expansion and profitability.

Key Principles of Growth Investing:

1. Focus on Growth Potential:

The core principle of growth investing is to identify companies with high growth potential. This could be due to emerging technologies, innovative products, expanding markets, or a strong competitive edge.

2. Momentum and Future Prospects:

Growth investors prioritize companies that are already experiencing momentum in terms of revenue and earnings growth. They assess a company's ability to maintain or accelerate this growth trajectory.

3. Long-Term Vision:

Growth investing often involves a long-term perspective. Investors believe that the potential for sustained growth over time will lead to substantial returns on their investments.

Methods of Growth Investing:

1. Earnings Growth Analysis:

Growth investors analyze a company's historical and projected earnings growth. Companies with a track record of consistent growth or those in industries with high growth potential are often favored.

2. Revenue Growth and Market Expansion:

Companies expanding into new markets or introducing innovative products have the potential for accelerated revenue growth, which attracts growth investors.

3. Competitive Advantage:

Investors seek companies with a competitive edge, whether through intellectual property, proprietary technology, or a dominant market position.

4. Industry Trends and Disruption:

Growth investors keep a close eye on emerging industry trends and disruptive technologies that can propel certain companies to the forefront.

Benefits of Growth Investing:

1. Potential for High Returns:

Successful growth investing can lead to significant capital appreciation as companies realize their growth potential and their stock prices increase.

2. Participating in Innovation:

Growth investors have the opportunity to invest in companies at the forefront of technological advancements and innovation.

3. Aligning with Market Trends:

Investors can align their portfolios with evolving market trends, positioning themselves to benefit from shifts in consumer behavior and industry dynamics.

4. Diversification:

Incorporating growth stocks into a diversified portfolio can balance risk by providing exposure to both growth and stability.

Challenges and Considerations:

1. High Valuations:

Growth stocks often trade at premium valuations due to high expectations. A sudden change in market sentiment can lead to price corrections.

2. Volatility:

The potential for high returns comes with increased volatility. Growth stocks can experience sharp price fluctuations in response to market news or sentiment.

3. Unpredictability:

Predicting which companies will successfully achieve their growth projections can be challenging, and not all high-growth prospects materialize.

4. Timing and Overvaluation:

Entering at the right time is crucial. Investing in growth stocks when they are overvalued might result in lower returns as the market corrects.

Growth investing is a strategy that seeks to identify companies poised for rapid earnings and revenue expansion. By focusing on innovation, competitive advantage, and market trends, growth investors aim to capitalize on the potential for significant capital appreciation. While it offers the allure of high returns, growth investing comes with increased risk and market volatility. Success in growth investing requires thorough research, an understanding of industry dynamics, and the ability to assess a company's long-term growth potential. As the financial landscape continues to evolve, growth investing remains a dynamic approach for investors who are willing to embrace change, innovation, and the promise of future opportunities.

3.5 Day Trading and Swing Trading

Day trading and swing trading are two popular trading strategies that focus on capitalizing on short-term price movements in financial markets. While both approaches involve relatively quick buying and selling of assets, they differ in terms of timeframes, strategies, and risk levels. This guide provides an in-depth exploration of day trading and swing trading, outlining their key principles, methods, benefits, and considerations.

Day Trading: Seizing Opportunities within a Single Day

Understanding Day Trading:

Day trading involves executing multiple trades within the same trading day, with the goal of profiting from intraday price fluctuations. Day traders do not hold positions overnight and aim to close all their trades by the end of the trading day. This strategy requires close attention to real-time market movements and quick decision-making.

Key Principles of Day Trading:

- **Intraday Focus**: Day traders focus exclusively on the intraday price movements of assets, capitalizing on short-lived trends and price swings.
- **Liquidity**: Liquidity is crucial in day trading. Traders prefer assets with high trading volumes and tight bid-ask spreads to ensure quick execution.
- **Risk Management**: Effective risk management is vital. Day traders often use stop-loss orders to limit potential losses.
- **Technical Analysis**: Technical indicators and chart patterns play a significant role in day trading decisions, as traders seek to predict short-term price movements.
- **Minimal Overnight Risk**: Since positions are closed by the end of the day, day traders avoid overnight market risk and news-driven price gaps.

Methods of Day Trading:

- **Scalping**: Scalpers make numerous quick trades throughout the day, aiming to profit from small price movements. Their focus is on capturing minimal price changes.

- **Momentum Trading**: Momentum traders capitalize on strong price trends and volume, entering positions in the direction of the prevailing momentum.
- **Breakout Trading**: Breakout traders look for assets that are breaking out of well-defined price ranges, seeking to profit from the continuation of the breakout movement.

Benefits of Day Trading:

- **Quick Profits**: Day trading provides the potential for rapid profits within a short timeframe, allowing traders to compound gains quickly.
- **No Overnight Risk**: Since positions are closed before the market closes, day traders are not exposed to overnight market events.
- **Focused Approach**: Day trading demands intense focus and concentration, which can be appealing to traders who enjoy making quick decisions.

Challenges and Considerations:

- **High Transaction Costs**: Frequent trading results in higher commission and fee expenses, which can eat into profits.
- **High Risk**: The fast-paced nature of day trading exposes traders to significant volatility and potential losses.
- **Emotional Stress**: The need to make quick decisions can lead to emotional trading and impulsive actions.
- **Swing Trading**: Capturing Short- to Medium-Term Trends

Understanding Swing Trading:

Swing trading aims to capture short- to medium-term price trends, typically holding positions for several days to weeks. Unlike day trading, swing traders do not need to make split-second decisions, allowing for more comprehensive analysis and reduced stress.

Key Principles of Swing Trading:

- **Technical Analysis**: Swing traders rely heavily on technical analysis, using chart patterns, indicators, and trendlines to identify potential entry and exit points.
- **Trend Identification**: Swing traders focus on identifying and riding established trends, aiming to profit from price movements within those trends.
- **Position Holding**: Unlike day traders, swing traders hold positions overnight and over weekends, allowing for more flexibility.
- **Risk Management**: Effective risk management is crucial in swing trading. Position sizing and stop-loss orders are commonly used to manage risk.

Methods of Swing Trading:

- **Trend Following**: Swing traders follow established trends and enter positions in the direction of the prevailing trend.
- **Counter-Trend Trading**: Some swing traders attempt to identify potential trend reversals and profit from short-term price corrections.

Benefits of Swing Trading:

- **Time Flexibility**: Swing traders can conduct thorough analysis and research without the need for split-second decision-making.
- **Reduced Stress**: Compared to day trading, swing trading offers a more relaxed approach with lower stress levels.
- **Potential for Substantial Gains**: Holding positions for several days to weeks provides the opportunity to capture larger price movements.

Challenges and Considerations:

- **Overnight Risk**: Holding positions overnight exposes swing traders to potential overnight market events and gaps.
- **Market Volatility**: While less intense than day trading, swing trading still involves exposure to market volatility and potential price reversals.
- **Time Commitment**: Although less time-sensitive than day trading, swing trading still requires consistent monitoring and analysis.

Day trading and swing trading are two distinct strategies that cater to traders with varying risk appetites, time commitments, and trading preferences. Day trading offers rapid potential profits within a single trading day, demanding quick decision-making and intense focus. On the other hand, swing trading provides the flexibility to capture short- to medium-term trends while allowing for more comprehensive analysis and reduced stress. Both approaches have their advantages and challenges, and choosing the right strategy depends on an individual's risk tolerance, time availability, and trading goals. Regardless of the chosen strategy, successful trading requires a solid understanding of market dynamics, risk management, and the ability to adapt to changing market conditions.

Chapter 4: Risk Management and Psychology

Effective risk management and a solid understanding of trading psychology are two critical components that underpin successful trading endeavors. Mastering these aspects is essential for traders and investors to navigate the dynamic and often unpredictable world of financial markets. This guide explores the vital concepts of risk management and trading psychology, highlighting their significance, strategies, and practical implications.

Risk Management: Safeguarding Capital and Long-Term Success

Understanding Risk Management:

Risk management is the process of identifying, assessing, and mitigating potential losses that can arise from trading activities. It's a systematic approach to protecting capital, maintaining consistency, and enhancing the longevity of trading ventures.

Key Principles of Risk Management:

- **Capital Preservation**: The primary goal of risk management is to protect capital from substantial losses, allowing traders to stay in the game even during adverse market conditions.
- **Risk-Reward Ratio**: This ratio determines the potential reward in relation to the amount risked on a trade. A favorable risk-reward ratio ensures that potential gains outweigh potential losses.

- **Position Sizing**: Determining the appropriate position size based on risk tolerance and the trade's risk-reward profile is crucial. Position sizes should be adjusted to align with the level of risk in each trade.
- **Diversification**: Spreading risk across multiple assets or trades can help reduce the impact of a single loss on the overall portfolio.
- **Stop-Loss Orders**: Placing stop-loss orders at predetermined levels helps limit potential losses by automatically closing positions if the price moves against the trade.

Risk Management Strategies:

- **Fixed Percentage Risk**: Traders risk a fixed percentage of their trading capital on each trade. This approach adjusts position size based on the trade's risk, maintaining consistent risk exposure.
- **Volatility-Based Position Sizing**: Position size is adjusted based on the asset's volatility. More volatile assets require smaller positions to account for larger potential price swings.
- **Portfolio Allocation**: Diversify the portfolio across different asset classes to reduce overall risk exposure.

Benefits of Effective Risk Management:

- **Capital Protection**: Effective risk management shields trading capital from excessive losses, preventing catastrophic impacts on the overall portfolio.
- **Consistency**: Consistent risk management promotes stable and predictable trading outcomes, reducing emotional decision-making.

- **Long-Term Sustainability**: By preventing significant drawdowns, risk management supports the longevity of trading activities and enhances the potential for long-term success.

Trading Psychology: Navigating Emotions and Decision-Making

Understanding Trading Psychology:

Trading psychology refers to the emotional and mental aspects that influence traders' decision-making processes. Emotions such as fear, greed, and overconfidence can significantly impact trading outcomes.

Key Psychological Factors:

- **Emotional Discipline**: Maintaining emotional discipline involves controlling the influence of emotions on trading decisions and avoiding impulsive actions.
- **Patience and Impulsiveness**: Successful traders exercise patience, waiting for the right setups rather than succumbing to the urge to trade frequently.
- **Overcoming Loss Aversion**: Losses are an inherent part of trading. Traders must learn to accept losses and avoid chasing them with risky trades.
- **Managing Fear and Greed**: Fear of missing out (FOMO) and greed can lead to irrational decisions. A balanced approach is crucial to avoid chasing market trends.

- **Adapting to Market Conditions**: Successful traders adapt their strategies to changing market conditions rather than clinging to fixed approaches.

Strategies for Managing Trading Psychology:

- **Mindfulness and Self-Awareness**: Developing self-awareness helps traders recognize emotional triggers and make more rational decisions.
- **Journaling**: Keeping a trading journal to record trades, emotions, and thought processes can provide insights into psychological patterns.
- **Taking Breaks**: Stepping away from the screens and taking breaks can help alleviate stress and prevent impulsive decisions.

Benefits of Mastering Trading Psychology:

- **Improved Decision-Making**: Emotionally disciplined traders make more rational decisions, avoiding impulsive actions driven by fear or greed.
- **Consistency**: Managing emotions promotes consistent trading performance and reduces the impact of emotional biases on trading outcomes.
- **Stress Reduction**: Psychological balance reduces stress, improving overall well-being and mental health.

Effective risk management and a strong understanding of trading psychology are foundational to achieving success in the world of trading and investing. By implementing risk management strategies, traders safeguard their capital, ensure consistency, and enhance their potential for sustainable profitability. Meanwhile, mastering trading psychology empowers traders to make rational decisions, navigate emotional challenges, and maintain a disciplined approach to trading. Combining these pillars—prudent risk management and a resilient psychological mindset—creates a strong foundation for traders to weather market fluctuations, capitalize on opportunities, and achieve their long-term financial goals.

4.1 Importance of Risk Management

In the realm of finance, risk is an ever-present companion that accompanies every investment, trade, and financial decision. The uncertainty inherent in financial markets can lead to both gains and losses, making effective risk management an indispensable element for individuals, businesses, and institutions alike. This comprehensive guide delves into the significance of risk management, its key principles, methods, benefits, and real-world implications, shedding light on its role in ensuring stability, longevity, and success in the complex world of finance.

Understanding Risk Management:

Risk management is a structured approach to identifying, assessing, mitigating, and monitoring potential risks that can impact the achievement of goals or objectives. It is a proactive strategy that seeks to minimize the negative effects of uncertainty while optimizing opportunities for positive outcomes. In the financial context, risk management encompasses various techniques and methodologies aimed at safeguarding capital, ensuring stability, and promoting consistent performance.

Key Principles of Risk Management:

- **Identification**: The first step in risk management involves identifying potential risks that can affect a project, investment, or business operation. These risks can range from market volatility and credit defaults to geopolitical events and regulatory changes.
- **Assessment**: Once risks are identified, they must be assessed in terms of their potential impact and likelihood of occurrence. This assessment helps prioritize risks and allocate resources effectively.
- **Mitigation**: Mitigation strategies involve taking proactive steps to reduce the impact or likelihood of risks. This can include diversification, hedging, insurance, and implementing robust internal controls.
- **Monitoring and Review**: Risk management is an ongoing process that requires continuous monitoring and periodic review. As market conditions and business environments evolve, risks can change, necessitating adjustments to mitigation strategies.

Methods of Risk Management:

- **Diversification**: Spreading investments across different asset classes, industries, and regions reduces the impact of a single event on the overall portfolio.
- **Hedging**: Using financial instruments such as options and futures to offset potential losses due to adverse price movements.

- **Insurance**: Purchasing insurance coverage to protect against specific risks, such as property damage, liability, or business interruption.
- **Capital Reserves**: Setting aside capital reserves to cover unexpected losses or financial emergencies.

The Significance of Risk Management:

1. Protection of Capital:

Effective risk management serves as a shield that protects capital from the detrimental impact of unforeseen events or adverse market conditions. By implementing strategies to mitigate potential losses, individuals and businesses can ensure their financial stability and longevity.

2. Consistency in Performance:

Risk management promotes consistency in performance by minimizing the impact of unexpected market fluctuations. A well-structured risk management strategy helps prevent drastic losses that can derail financial goals.

3. Decision-Making Clarity:

By identifying and assessing potential risks, individuals and businesses can make informed and rational decisions. This clarity aids in avoiding impulsive actions driven by fear, greed, or market sentiment.

4. Regulatory Compliance:

In regulated industries, risk management is often a legal requirement. Compliance with risk management standards not only avoids legal issues but also demonstrates a commitment to responsible business practices.

5. Longevity and Sustainability:

Effective risk management contributes to the longevity and sustainability of businesses and investments. A resilient approach to risk ensures the ability to weather economic downturns and capitalize on opportunities.

Real-World Implications:

1. Financial Institutions:

Banks and financial institutions are at the forefront of risk management. They assess credit risk, market risk, operational risk, and other factors to ensure the stability of their operations and protect depositors' funds.

2. Corporations:

Corporations manage risks related to supply chain disruptions, regulatory changes, and market volatility to maintain consistent operations and shareholder value.

3. Investors:

Individual investors employ risk management strategies to protect their investments from market downturns and ensure their financial security over the long term.

4. Government Entities:

Government agencies manage risks associated with public policies, economic fluctuations, and geopolitical events to ensure the stability and growth of their nations' economies.

Benefits of Effective Risk Management:

- **Minimized Losses**: Effective risk management minimizes the impact of potential losses, preserving capital and financial stability.
- **Enhanced Decision-Making**: Rational decision-making is promoted when potential risks are identified and assessed, allowing for better choices in uncertain situations.

- **Long-Term Sustainability**: A robust risk management strategy ensures the long-term viability of investments, businesses, and financial operations.
- **Stability and Reliability**: Businesses and institutions that implement sound risk management practices are perceived as stable, reliable, and trustworthy.

Challenges and Considerations:

- **Uncertainty**: The dynamic and unpredictable nature of financial markets makes risk assessment and management complex.
- **Costs**: Implementing risk management strategies can involve costs, including insurance premiums, hedging expenses, and research expenditures.
- **Overconfidence**: Overestimating the effectiveness of risk management strategies can lead to complacency and inadequate preparation for potential risks.

Risk management is not merely a precautionary measure; it is a fundamental principle that underpins successful ventures in the financial landscape. Whether applied by individuals, corporations, or governments, effective risk management strategies offer protection, stability, and the means to capitalize on opportunities while navigating uncertain terrain. By identifying, assessing, mitigating, and monitoring potential risks, individuals and businesses can safeguard their financial interests, promote consistent performance, and ensure their sustained success in the dynamic and ever-evolving world of finance.

4.2 Emotions and Trading Decisions

The realm of finance, characterized by its complex interplay of data, trends, and market forces, is intrinsically intertwined with the realm of human emotions. Every decision made in the financial landscape—whether it's an investment, trade, or strategic move—is influenced by the psychological factors that underpin human behavior. This comprehensive guide delves into the intricate relationship between emotions and trading decisions, exploring the key emotions at play, their impact on decision-making, strategies for managing emotions, and the significance of maintaining a balanced psychological mindset in the world of finance.

The Role of Emotions in Trading:

Emotions are an inherent part of human nature, and they inevitably find their way into the decision-making processes of traders and investors. The two primary emotions that heavily influence trading decisions are fear and greed. Fear arises from the anticipation of loss, while greed stems from the desire for profit. These emotions, if not managed effectively, can lead to impulsive and irrational decisions that can have a significant impact on trading outcomes.

Impact of Emotions on Trading Decisions:

- **Fear**: Fear often leads to hesitation, reluctance to take risks, and premature exits from trades. Traders driven by fear may miss out on profitable opportunities or exit trades too early, preventing them from maximizing their gains.

- **Greed**: Greed can result in overconfidence and risk-taking beyond one's risk tolerance. Traders driven by greed might take overly aggressive positions, ignore risk management strategies, and chase unrealistic profits.
- **Impulsivity**: Emotional decision-making can lead to impulsive actions without proper analysis or consideration of consequences. This can result in entering trades that don't align with a trading strategy.
- **Loss Aversion**: Traders may become overly focused on avoiding losses, leading them to hold losing positions for too long, hoping they will turn profitable. This behavior can lead to further losses.
- **Confirmation Bias**: Emotional bias can lead traders to seek out information that confirms their preconceived notions while ignoring contradictory data.

Strategies for Managing Emotions:

- **Mindfulness and Self-Awareness**: Developing self-awareness allows traders to recognize their emotional triggers and make more rational decisions.
- **Education and Knowledge**: Acquiring knowledge about market dynamics and trading strategies can boost confidence and reduce emotional reactions.
- **Trading Plans**: Creating and sticking to a well-defined trading plan helps reduce emotional decision-making by providing a structured approach.
- **Setting Realistic Goals**: Establishing achievable goals and expectations helps prevent the allure of chasing unrealistic profits.

- **Journaling**: Keeping a trading journal to document emotions, thoughts, and trade outcomes can provide insights into psychological patterns.

Psychological Pitfalls to Avoid:

- **Overconfidence**: Believing that you're immune to emotional biases can lead to overconfidence, causing you to ignore rational analysis.
- **Chasing Losses**: Trying to recover losses by taking risky trades can exacerbate losses and emotional distress.
- **Ignoring Analysis**: Relying solely on emotions to make trading decisions without proper analysis can lead to suboptimal outcomes.
- **Herd Mentality**: Following the crowd without independent analysis can lead to trading decisions influenced by market sentiment rather than rationality.

Maintaining a Balanced Psychological Mindset:

- Patience: Successful traders exercise patience, waiting for favorable setups rather than succumbing to the pressure of constant action.
- Discipline: Adhering to a well-defined trading plan and risk management strategies helps maintain discipline in the face of emotional challenges.
- Resilience: Accepting that losses are a natural part of trading helps build emotional resilience and prevents impulsive actions.Adaptability: Adapting to changing market conditions and

learning from mistakes is crucial for maintaining a balanced mindset.

The Significance of Psychological Balance:

Maintaining a balanced psychological mindset is paramount for successful trading. Emotions can amplify the impact of market volatility and lead to irrational decision-making. Conversely, a calm and rational approach allows traders to make informed choices, manage risks effectively, and capitalize on opportunities without being swayed by emotional biases.

Emotions are an inseparable part of the human experience, and trading decisions are no exception. Recognizing the influence of emotions, understanding their impact on decision-making, and implementing strategies to manage them are crucial steps for achieving success in the world of finance. By developing self-awareness, adhering to trading plans, and maintaining a balanced psychological mindset, traders can navigate the complexities of financial markets with confidence, resilience, and a higher likelihood of achieving their trading goals.

4.3 Developing a Disciplined Mindset

In the world of finance, a disciplined mindset is the cornerstone of success. It's the mental framework that empowers traders, investors, and financial professionals to make rational decisions, stick to strategies, and navigate the complexities of the market with resilience. Developing and nurturing a disciplined mindset is not just a choice—it's a conscious effort to cultivate habits, attitudes, and practices that lead to consistent success. This guide delves into the importance of a disciplined mindset, strategies to foster discipline, and the profound impact it has on achieving financial goals.

Understanding the Disciplined Mindset:

A disciplined mindset is characterized by a set of mental traits, behaviors, and practices that prioritize consistency, rationality, and long-term goals over short-term impulses and emotional reactions. It involves the ability to adhere to predetermined strategies, manage emotions, and maintain a sense of self-control, even in the face of adversity.

Key Elements of a Disciplined Mindset:

- **Patience**: A disciplined mindset recognizes the value of patience. It involves waiting for the right opportunities, rather than chasing quick wins.
- **Consistency**: Consistency is the bedrock of discipline. It involves adhering to a well-defined trading plan, strategy, or investment approach over time.
- **Emotional Regulation**: A disciplined mindset acknowledges and manages emotions, preventing them from driving impulsive or irrational decisions.
- **Self-Awareness**: Developing self-awareness allows individuals to recognize their strengths, weaknesses, and emotional triggers, facilitating better decision-making.
- **Adaptability**: While consistency is vital, a disciplined mindset also recognizes the need to adapt strategies when market conditions change.

Strategies to Foster Discipline:

- **Establish Clear Goals**: Clearly defined financial goals provide direction and motivation, anchoring your decisions in a long-term perspective.
- **Create a Trading Plan**: A comprehensive trading plan outlines strategies, risk management, and guidelines, reducing the influence of impulsive decisions.
- **Set Rules and Boundaries**: Establish specific rules for entry and exit points, position sizes, and risk tolerance, and stick to them rigorously.
- **Practice Self-Control**: Develop self-control by resisting the urge to act on emotions. This might involve stepping away from the computer during periods of high stress.
- **Avoid Chasing Losses**: Recognize that losses are part of the game. Avoid chasing losses by sticking to your plan and refraining from emotional trading.
- **Review and Learn**: Regularly review your trades and investment decisions to learn from mistakes and refine your approach.

The Profound Impact of Discipline:

- **Consistency in Performance**: A disciplined mindset leads to consistent performance, which is essential for achieving long-term financial goals.
- **Rational Decision-Making**: Disciplined individuals make decisions based on analysis and strategy rather than being swayed by emotions.

- **Emotional Resilience**: Developing emotional resilience allows you to handle losses, setbacks, and market volatility without making hasty decisions.
- **Adaptation to Market Changes**: A disciplined approach fosters the ability to adapt to changing market conditions while staying true to core strategies.
- **Long-Term Success**: Discipline is the linchpin of long-term success. It prevents the pitfalls of short-term thinking and impulsive actions.

Challenges and Considerations:

- **Emotional Biases**: Emotional biases can challenge even the most disciplined individuals. Recognizing and managing these biases is crucial.
- **Temptation of Quick Wins**: The allure of quick profits can tempt traders to deviate from their disciplined strategies. Staying committed is essential.
- **Market Volatility**: Maintaining discipline during times of high market volatility can be particularly challenging. Emotional control is vital.

A disciplined mindset is not a one-time accomplishment; it's an ongoing journey of self-improvement and growth. It requires self-awareness, commitment, and the willingness to learn from mistakes. By prioritizing consistency, rationality, and emotional regulation, individuals can foster a disciplined mindset that forms the bedrock of their success in the financial landscape. Whether you're a seasoned trader, an investor, or someone just entering the world of finance, cultivating and nurturing a disciplined mindset will prove to be your most valuable asset in achieving your financial aspirations.

Chapter 5: Getting Started with Stock Trading

Stock trading, with its potential for financial growth and the thrill of participating in the dynamic world of markets, is an appealing venture for many individuals. However, stepping into the realm of stock trading requires careful preparation, understanding, and a solid foundation of knowledge. This guide serves as your compass, offering essential insights and actionable steps to help you embark on your stock trading journey with confidence and informed decision-making.

Understanding the Basics:

- **Learn the Language**: Familiarize yourself with stock market terminology, including terms like stocks, shares, dividends, market orders, and more. This foundational knowledge will help you communicate effectively and navigate the trading landscape.
- **Grasp the Concept of Stocks**: Stocks represent ownership in a company. When you buy shares of a company's stock, you become a partial owner and have the potential to benefit from its profits and growth.
- **Recognize Market Exchanges**: Stock trading takes place on exchanges such as the New York Stock Exchange (NYSE) or the Nasdaq. These platforms facilitate the buying and selling of stocks.
- **Understand the Market**: Stock prices are influenced by supply and demand dynamics, company performance, economic factors, and investor sentiment. Learning how these factors interact will give you insight into price movements.
- **Define Your Trading Goals**: Determine whether you're looking for short-term gains (trading) or long-term growth (investing). Your goals will shape your strategies and approach.

Preparing for Trading:

- **Educate Yourself**: Knowledge is your most valuable asset. Read books, attend online courses, watch educational videos, and stay up to date with financial news to build a solid foundation.
- **Set Up a Trading Account**: Choose a reputable brokerage platform to open a trading account. Look for user-friendly interfaces, reasonable fees, and a variety of research tools.
- **Develop a Trading Plan**: Define your trading strategy, risk tolerance, and goals. Determine how much capital you're willing to invest and how much risk you're comfortable taking on each trade.
- **Practice with Virtual Trading**: Many brokerage platforms offer virtual trading accounts where you can practice trading with virtual money. This helps you get comfortable with the platform and your strategies before using real money.
- **Learn Technical and Fundamental Analysis**: These are two key approaches to analyzing stocks. Technical analysis involves studying price charts and patterns, while fundamental analysis examines a company's financial health and market position.

Starting Your Trading Journey:

- **Begin with Small Positions**: Start with small investments as you get a feel for the market and gain confidence in your strategies.
- **Focus on Quality Research**: Thoroughly research the companies you're interested in. Consider their financials, industry trends, competitive advantages, and growth potential.
- **Practice Patience**: Trading is not about constant action. Be patient and wait for opportunities that align with your strategies.

- **Embrace Risk Management**: Protect your capital by setting stop-loss orders to limit potential losses and avoid overextending yourself.
- **Continuously Learn and Adapt**: The stock market is dynamic and ever-changing. Stay curious, keep learning, and be willing to adapt your strategies based on new information.

Managing Your Emotions:

- **Control Your Emotions**: Emotions can lead to impulsive decisions. Practice emotional discipline by sticking to your trading plan and avoiding rash actions.
- **Accept Losses**: Losses are a natural part of trading. Accept them as learning opportunities and don't let them deter you from your goals.
- **Stay Balanced**: Maintaining a balanced mindset helps you make rational decisions, even when faced with market volatility.

Embarking on your stock trading journey requires a blend of knowledge, discipline, and a willingness to learn from experience. With the right preparation, a well-defined trading plan, and a commitment to continuous improvement, you can navigate the complexities of the stock market and work toward your financial aspirations. Remember that trading involves risks, and while there's potential for significant gains, there's also the possibility of losses. Stay patient, stay informed, and stay focused on your goals as you take your first steps in the exciting world of stock trading.

5.1 Setting up a Trading Account

Setting up a trading account is the crucial first step on your journey to participating in the dynamic world of financial markets. Whether you're interested in stocks, forex, commodities, or other instruments, a trading account provides you with the platform and tools to execute trades, manage your investments, and potentially achieve your financial goals. This guide outlines the essential steps to establish a trading account, highlighting key considerations and factors to ensure you start your trading journey on the right foot.

Understanding Trading Accounts:

A trading account is a specialized account offered by brokerage firms that allows you to buy, sell, and trade various financial instruments. These instruments can include stocks, bonds, currencies, commodities, and more, depending on the type of account and the brokerage's offerings.

Choosing a Brokerage Firm:

Selecting the right brokerage is crucial for a seamless trading experience. Consider the following factors:

- **Regulation**: Ensure the brokerage is regulated by a reputable financial authority. Regulatory oversight offers investor protection and adherence to industry standards.

- **Fees and Commissions**: Different brokerages have varying fee structures. Compare commission rates, spreads, and any additional charges associated with trading.
- **Trading Platform**: The trading platform is the interface through which you execute trades. It should be user-friendly, reliable, and offer the features you need.
- **Asset Variety**: Depending on your trading preferences, choose a brokerage that offers the financial instruments you're interested in trading.
- **Research and Analysis Tools**: Look for a platform that provides access to research reports, market analysis, and real-time data to inform your trading decisions.

Opening a Trading Account:

Once you've chosen a brokerage, follow these steps to open a trading account:

- **Online Application**: Most brokerages offer an online account application process. Provide your personal information, contact details, and any required documentation.
- **Verification**: Your identity and documents will need to be verified to comply with regulatory standards. This can involve submitting government-issued identification, proof of address, and financial information.
- **Choose Account Type**: Brokerages often offer different types of accounts, such as individual accounts, joint accounts, retirement accounts, and more. Select the one that aligns with your needs.

- **Deposit Funds**: Fund your trading account by transferring money from your bank account to the trading account. Many brokerages offer various funding methods, including bank transfers, credit/debit cards, and online payment platforms.
- **Terms and Conditions**: Review and agree to the terms and conditions of the brokerage. This includes understanding their fee structure, trading policies, and client agreements.
- **Account Approval**: After your account application is reviewed and approved, you'll receive confirmation and access to your trading platform.

Navigating Your Trading Account:

Once your trading account is set up, you'll have access to various tools and features:

- **Trading Platform**: Explore the trading platform's features, including order placement, charting tools, technical indicators, and real-time market data.
- **Research and Analysis**: Utilize research tools to analyze market trends, news, and company information to make informed trading decisions.
- **Funding and Withdrawals**: Fund your account and manage your funds through the platform. You can also request withdrawals when needed.
- **Education**: Many brokerages offer educational resources, webinars, and tutorials to help you improve your trading skills.

- **Customer Support**: Familiarize yourself with the customer support options available in case you have questions or encounter issues.

Risk Management and Trading Practices:

Before you start trading, it's essential to establish risk management practices:

- **Risk Tolerance**: Define your risk tolerance based on your financial situation, investment goals, and comfort level with potential losses.
- **Position Sizing**: Determine how much of your capital you'll allocate to each trade. Avoid risking too much on a single trade.
- **Stop-Loss Orders**: Set stop-loss orders to limit potential losses on your trades. This helps protect your capital.
- **Trading Plan**: Develop a trading plan that outlines your strategies, goals, and risk management rules. Stick to your plan to avoid impulsive decisions.

Setting up a trading account is the gateway to your journey in financial markets. It's a step that requires careful consideration of factors such as brokerage reputation, account types, fees, and trading platform features. With the right brokerage and a well-defined trading plan, you'll have the tools you need to explore the world of trading, make informed decisions, and work toward your financial objectives. Remember that trading involves risks, and thorough preparation and continuous learning are essential for a successful trading experience.

5.2 Choosing a Brokerage Platform

Selecting the right brokerage platform is a pivotal decision that can significantly impact your trading journey. A brokerage platform serves as your gateway to the financial markets, providing access to trading tools, research resources, and execution capabilities. With a multitude of options available, it's essential to navigate the choices carefully to find a platform that aligns with your trading goals and preferences. This guide walks you through the crucial factors to consider when choosing a brokerage platform, empowering you to make an informed decision that sets the stage for successful trading.

Factors to Consider When Choosing a Brokerage Platform:

1. **Regulation and Reputation:**

Ensure the brokerage is regulated by a reputable financial authority. Regulation provides investor protection and ensures adherence to industry standards. Research the brokerage's reputation, reviews, and track record to gauge its credibility.

2. **Trading Fees and Costs:**

Compare the fee structure of different platforms. This includes commissions, spreads, and any additional charges associated with trading. Consider how fees may impact your trading profitability, especially for frequent traders.

3. Trading Instruments:

Determine which financial instruments you plan to trade—stocks, forex, commodities, cryptocurrencies, etc. Choose a platform that offers a wide range of instruments or specializes in the specific markets you're interested in.

4. Trading Platform and Technology:

Evaluate the trading platform's features, ease of use, and reliability. A user-friendly platform with intuitive navigation, advanced charting tools, technical indicators, and real-time market data is essential for effective trading.

5. Execution Speed and Reliability:

Timely execution of trades is crucial. Choose a platform known for its fast and reliable order execution, minimizing the risk of slippage and missed opportunities.

6. Research and Analysis Tools:

Access to research reports, market analysis, economic calendars, and real-time data can significantly enhance your decision-making process. A robust research toolkit helps you stay informed about market trends and news.

7. Customer Support:

Reliable customer support is essential for resolving issues, addressing queries, and navigating platform-related challenges. Ensure the brokerage offers accessible and responsive customer support channels.

8. Mobile Trading:

If you prefer trading on the go, consider whether the platform offers a mobile app. Mobile trading allows you to monitor markets, execute trades, and manage your portfolio from your smartphone or tablet.

9. Educational Resources:

Look for brokerages that provide educational resources such as webinars, tutorials, articles, and guides. Learning materials can help you improve your trading skills and stay updated on market trends.

10. Demo Account Availability:

Some brokerages offer demo accounts that allow you to practice trading with virtual money. This is a valuable feature for new traders to familiarize themselves with the platform before using real funds.

11. Account Types and Options:

Explore the different account types offered by the brokerage, such as individual accounts, joint accounts, retirement accounts, and more. Choose the one that aligns with your trading needs.

Steps to Evaluate Brokerage Platforms:

1. Research and Compare:

Research multiple brokerage platforms and create a comparison chart that highlights key features, fees, and available instruments.

2. Read Reviews and Testimonials:

Read reviews and testimonials from other traders to gain insights into their experiences with the platforms you're considering.

3. Check Regulation and Compliance:

Verify the brokerage's regulatory status and ensure it complies with relevant financial authorities.

4. Explore the Platform's Demo:

If available, explore the platform's demo version to familiarize yourself with its interface and features.

5. Contact Customer Support:

Reach out to customer support with questions or concerns to gauge their responsiveness and professionalism.

6. Consider Your Trading Style:

Your trading style—day trading, swing trading, long-term investing—will influence the platform features you require.

Choosing a brokerage platform is a crucial decision that impacts your trading experience and potential success. By carefully evaluating factors such as regulation, fees, technology, research tools, and customer support, you can make an informed choice that aligns with your trading goals and preferences. Remember that your chosen platform serves as the foundation for your trading journey, so invest time and effort in selecting the one that empowers you to navigate the financial markets with confidence and precision.

5.3 Placing Orders and Executing Trades

Placing orders and executing trades are the fundamental actions that enable you to participate in the dynamic world of financial markets. These actions are the heart of trading, allowing you to buy and sell various financial instruments such as stocks, currencies, commodities, and more. Mastering the process of placing orders and executing trades is essential for effective trading and achieving your financial goals. This guide provides you with a comprehensive overview of how to place orders, execute trades, and navigate the intricacies of the trading process.

Understanding Order Types:

Before you execute a trade, you need to understand the different types of orders:

1. **Market Order**: A market order is an instruction to buy or sell an asset immediately at the current market price. Market orders offer quick execution but do not guarantee a specific price.
2. **Limit Order**: A limit order is placed with a specific price at which you're willing to buy or sell an asset. It will be executed only if the market reaches the specified price.
3. **Stop Order**: A stop order becomes a market order when a specific price is reached. A buy stop is placed above the current market price, and a sell stop is placed below it.
4. **Stop-Limit Order**: Similar to a stop order, a stop-limit order becomes a limit order when a specific price is reached. It combines the features of a stop order and a limit order.

Placing Orders:

1. **Log into Your Trading Account**: Access your brokerage platform using your credentials.
2. **Choose the Asset**: Select the financial instrument you want to trade (e.g., stocks, forex pairs, commodities).
3. **Select the Order Type**: Choose the appropriate order type based on your trading strategy and goals.
4. **Enter Order Details**:

- **For market orders**: Specify the quantity (number of units or shares).
- **For limit orders**: Specify the price at which you want the order to be executed.
- **For stop orders**: Specify the trigger price and the order price.
- **Review and Confirm**: Carefully review the order details, including the order type, quantity, and price. Once you're satisfied, confirm the order.

Executing Trades:

Once you've placed an order, the execution process begins:

1. **Immediate Execution (Market Orders):**

- Market orders are executed instantly at the prevailing market price.
- The execution price may vary slightly from the price displayed at the time of order placement due to market fluctuations.

2. **Price-Triggered Execution (Limit and Stop Orders):**

- Limit orders are executed when the market reaches the specified price.
- Stop orders are triggered when the market reaches the specified trigger price. They then become market or limit orders, depending on the type.

Monitoring and Managing Trades:

1. **Monitor Open Orders**: Keep track of your open orders through your trading platform. You can see whether they have been executed, canceled, or are still pending.
2. **Modify or Cancel Orders**: You can modify or cancel pending orders if market conditions change or if you decide to adjust your strategy.
3. **Set Stop-Loss and Take-Profit Levels**: As a risk management strategy, set stop-loss orders to limit potential losses and take-profit orders to secure profits at specified levels.
4. **Track Market Movement**: Monitor market trends, news, and price movements that could impact your trades. This information can help you make informed decisions.

Risk Management and Discipline:

1. **Position Sizing**: Determine the appropriate size of your trade based on your risk tolerance and trading strategy.
2. **Risk-Reward Ratio**: Assess the potential reward against the risk of your trade. Aim for a favorable risk-reward ratio.
3. **Stay Disciplined**: Stick to your trading plan, avoid emotional decisions, and maintain consistent risk management practices.

Placing orders and executing trades are the core actions that translate your trading strategies into reality. By understanding the different order types, placing orders correctly, and effectively managing your trades, you can navigate the financial markets with confidence and precision. Remember that successful trading involves thorough preparation, continuous learning, and a disciplined approach to risk management. With practice and experience, you can develop the skills needed to execute trades that align with your financial goals and contribute to your trading success.

5.4 Building a Diversified Portfolio

Building a diversified portfolio is a strategic approach to investing that aims to reduce risk and enhance potential returns by spreading investments across a range of different assets. A well-diversified portfolio is like a sturdy fortress, with each asset acting as a building block to create a foundation of stability and growth. This guide outlines the importance of diversification, strategies for constructing a diversified portfolio, and the benefits it offers to investors seeking to achieve their financial objectives.

Understanding Diversification:

Diversification is the practice of allocating investments across a variety of asset classes, industries, sectors, and geographic regions. The goal is to mitigate the impact of poor performance in any single asset, providing a buffer against market volatility and enhancing the likelihood of consistent returns.

Key Benefits of a Diversified Portfolio:

- **Risk Reduction**: By spreading investments, you minimize the impact of a single investment's poor performance on your overall portfolio.
- **Potential for Stable Returns**: A well-diversified portfolio can generate more stable returns over time, even if individual assets experience fluctuations.
- **Enhanced Risk-Return Tradeoff**: Diversification allows you to balance risk and potential reward by investing in assets with varying levels of risk and return potential.
- **Adaptability**: A diverse portfolio can better withstand changes in market conditions, economic shifts, and unexpected events.

Strategies for Building a Diversified Portfolio:

- **Asset Allocation**: Allocate your investments across different asset classes, such as stocks, bonds, cash, and alternative investments like real estate or commodities.
- **Geographic Diversification**: Invest in companies and assets from various regions and countries to reduce exposure to specific economic and political risks.
- **Industry and Sector Allocation**: Diversify within the equity portion of your portfolio by investing in different industries and sectors.
- **Investment Styles**: Include assets that represent various investment styles, such as value, growth, or income-oriented securities.
- **Market Capitalization**: Invest in companies of varying market capitalizations, including large-cap, mid-cap, and small-cap stocks.

- **Fixed-Income Assets**: Incorporate bonds with different maturities, credit qualities, and interest rate sensitivities to balance the risk profile.
- **Alternative Investments**: Consider adding alternative investments like real estate, commodities, or hedge funds to add further diversification.

Implementing Diversification:

- **Assess Risk Tolerance**: Understand your risk tolerance and investment goals to guide your diversification strategy.
- **Set Portfolio Targets**: Determine the desired allocation percentages for each asset class based on your risk profile and goals.
- **Regular Rebalancing**: Monitor your portfolio regularly and rebalance as needed to maintain your desired asset allocation. Rebalancing involves selling assets that have been appreciated and buying those that have underperformed.
- **Stay Informed**: Keep up with market trends, economic indicators, and industry news to make informed adjustments to your portfolio.

Potential Considerations:

- **Over-Diversification**: While diversification is crucial, over-diversification can lead to diluted returns and complexity in managing the portfolio.
- **Correlation**: Consider the correlation between assets; some may move in similar directions during market movements, reducing the benefits of diversification.

- **Risk Assessment**: Understand that diversification cannot eliminate all risks; it aims to reduce specific risks associated with individual assets.

Building a diversified portfolio is a strategic approach that reflects careful consideration of your risk tolerance, investment objectives, and market insights. By diversifying across different asset classes, regions, industries, and investment styles, you create a well-balanced foundation for financial growth and stability. Diversification is not a one-time task; it requires periodic assessment and adjustments to align with changing market conditions and you're evolving financial goals. As you construct and manage your diversified portfolio, you position yourself to navigate the complexities of the financial markets with confidence and resilience, striving toward your long-term investment objectives.

Chapter 6: Advanced Trading Techniques

As traders gain experience and confidence in their abilities, they often seek to delve into advanced trading techniques that go beyond the basics. These techniques are designed to provide traders with a competitive edge, allowing them to capitalize on market inefficiencies, manage risk more effectively, and adapt to changing market conditions. This guide explores a range of advanced trading techniques, including algorithmic trading, options strategies, short selling, margin trading, and more. By understanding and incorporating these techniques into their trading arsenal, experienced traders can enhance their potential for success in the dynamic world of financial markets.

Algorithmic Trading:

Algorithmic trading, often referred to as algo trading, involves the use of computer algorithms to execute trades based on predefined criteria. This technique offers several advantages, including:

- **Speed**: Algorithms can execute trades at lightning speed, taking advantage of market opportunities in milliseconds.
- **Accuracy**: Algos eliminates human errors and emotions, ensuring trades are executed exactly as planned.
- **Complex Strategies**: Advanced algorithms can execute complex trading strategies that involve multiple variables and conditions.
- **Arbitrage Opportunities**: Algorithms can identify and exploit price discrepancies between different markets or assets.

Options Strategies:

Options trading involves contracts that give traders the right (but not the obligation) to buy or sell an asset at a predetermined price within a specified timeframe. Advanced options strategies include:

- **Straddle**: Simultaneously buying a call and a put option with the same strike price and expiration date. It profits from significant price fluctuations.
- **Iron Condor**: Combines a bear call spread and a bull put spread to generate income in a range-bound market.
- **Butterfly Spread**: Involves three strike prices to profit from low volatility scenarios.

Short Selling:

Short selling is the practice of selling borrowed shares with the expectation that their price will decline, allowing the trader to buy them back at a lower price and make a profit. Advanced short-selling techniques include:

- **Pairs Trading**: Simultaneously short-selling one stock and longing for another in the same sector, capitalizing on price divergences.
- **Convertible Arbitrage**: Shorting a company's convertible bonds while buying the underlying stock.

Margin Trading:

Margin trading allows traders to borrow funds from a broker to increase their trading position. It amplifies potential gains but also increases potential losses. Advanced margin trading techniques include:

- **Leveraged ETFs**: Trading leveraged exchange-traded funds (ETFs) that aim to amplify market movements.
- **Portfolio Margin**: A risk-based margin approach that factors in the correlation between positions to determine margin requirements.

Swing Trading:

Swing trading involves holding positions for several days to weeks, capitalizing on short- to medium-term price movements. Advanced swing trading techniques include:

- **Fibonacci Retracements**: Using Fibonacci levels to identify potential support and resistance levels for price reversals.
- **Moving Average Crossovers**: Utilizing moving averages of different periods to identify trends and entry/exit points.

Day Trading:

Day trading involves executing multiple trades within a single trading day. Advanced day trading techniques include:

- **Scalping**: Making rapid, small trades to profit from minor price fluctuations.
- **Volume Analysis**: Analyzing trading volume patterns to identify potential price movements.

Hedging Strategies:

Hedging involves taking positions to mitigate the risk of adverse price movements. Advanced hedging techniques include:

- **Delta Hedging**: Adjusting options positions to ensure minimal exposure to changes in the underlying asset's price.
- **Cross-Hedging**: Using correlated assets to hedge positions in related markets.

Pair Trading:

Pair trading involves simultaneously taking long and short positions in two correlated instruments to profit from relative price changes. Advanced pair trading techniques include:

- **Cointegration**: Identifying pairs that exhibit a long-term relationship, allowing traders to capture price deviations.

Market Sentiment Analysis:

Market sentiment analysis involves assessing investor emotions to gauge potential price movements. Advanced sentiment analysis techniques include:

- **Social Media Monitoring**: Analyzing social media platforms for real-time market sentiment trends.
- **News Analysis**: Identifying market-moving news and understanding its impact on asset prices.

Risk Management and Psychology:

While exploring advanced trading techniques, maintaining effective risk management practices and emotional discipline remains paramount. Consider advanced risk management techniques such as using options to hedge positions or employing dynamic position sizing strategies.

Advanced trading techniques offer experienced traders a toolkit to enhance their trading strategies and navigate the complexities of financial markets. It's crucial to approach these techniques with a solid understanding, continuous learning, and a commitment to disciplined risk management. While these techniques provide opportunities for potential gains, they also involve increased complexity and risk. By incorporating advanced techniques into a comprehensive trading plan and adapting them to market conditions, experienced traders can strive for greater consistency, adaptability, and success in their trading endeavors.

6.1 Options Trading Strategies

Options trading offers a versatile range of strategies that allow traders to capitalize on various market conditions and objectives. Whether you're aiming to profit from price movements, generate income, or hedge against risk, options can be powerful tools in your trading arsenal. This guide provides an overview of some popular options trading strategies, each designed to address specific market scenarios and goals.

1. **Long Call:**

Objective: Profit from upward price movements.

Execution: Buy a call option, giving you the right to buy the underlying asset at a predetermined price (strike price) within a specified time (expiration).

2. **Long Put:**

Objective: Profit from downward price movements.

Execution: Buy a put option, granting you the right to sell the underlying asset at a predetermined price within a specified time.

3. **Covered Call:**

Objective: Generate income from a position you already own.

Execution: Sell a call option against a long stock position you hold. If the price rises, you'll still profit up to the strike price, but you won't benefit from prices above that level.

4.   Protective Put:

Objective: Hedge against potential losses.

Execution: Buy a put option as insurance against a drop in the value of your stock holdings. If the stock price falls, the put option's value increases, offsetting losses in the stock.

5.   Long Straddle:

Objective: Profit from significant price movements, regardless of direction.

Execution: Simultaneously buy a call and a put option with the same strike price and expiration. If the price moves significantly, one option's gains can offset the other's losses.

6.   Long Strangle:

Objective: Profit from significant price movements, with a wider range than the straddle.

Execution: Buy an out-of-the-money call and an out-of-the-money put option. While risk is lower compared to a straddle, price movement is required to profit.

7. Iron Condor:

Objective: Profit in a range-bound market.

Execution: Combine a bear call spread (selling a call at a lower strike price and buying a call at a higher strike) with a bull put spread (selling a put at a higher strike and buying a put at a lower strike).

8. Butterfly Spread:

Objective: Profit from low volatility.

Execution: Combine both a long and a short straddle, with the short straddle having a higher strike price than the long straddle.

9. Calendar Spread:

Objective: Benefit from time decay.

Execution: Buy an option with a longer expiration date and simultaneously sell an option with a nearer expiration. As time passes, the near-month option loses value faster than the far-month option.

10. Ratio Spread:

Objective: Profit from price movements with limited risk.

Execution: Combine options of differing quantities and strikes to create a spread that can lead to higher potential returns.

11. Collar:

Objective: Protect profits while limiting downside risk.

Execution: Buy a protective put option and simultaneously sell a covered call. This strategy can cap both potential gains and losses.

12. Synthetic Positions:

Objective: Replicate a stock position with lower capital requirements.

Execution: Combine call and put options to mimic the effects of owning the underlying stock.

Options trading strategies offer traders a range of tools to adapt to different market conditions, achieve various objectives, and manage risk effectively. It's crucial to thoroughly understand each strategy's mechanics, risks, and potential rewards before implementing them in your trading plan. As with any trading approach, ongoing learning, practice, and risk management are essential for success. By incorporating suitable options strategies into your trading repertoire, you can enhance your ability to navigate the complexities of financial markets and work toward your trading goals.

6.2 Futures Trading

Futures trading is a dynamic and advanced approach that allows traders to speculate on the future price of various underlying assets, including commodities, currencies, stock indexes, and interest rates. It involves entering into contracts obligating traders to buy or sell these assets at predetermined prices on specified future dates. Futures trading offers potential benefits such as risk management, hedging, and speculation. This guide provides an overview of futures trading, its mechanics, strategies, and considerations for those interested in exploring this sophisticated trading avenue.

Understanding Futures Contracts:

A futures contract is a standardized agreement between two parties to buy or sell a specific quantity of an underlying asset at a predetermined price (the futures price) on a specified future date. Key elements of a futures contract include:

- **Underlying Asset**: The asset being traded, which can range from commodities like gold and oil to financial instruments like stock indexes.
- **Futures Price**: The price at which the contract will be executed on the future settlement date.
- **Expiration Date**: The date on which the contract matures and the parties fulfill their obligations.

Benefits of Futures Trading:

- **Risk Management**: Futures contracts allow hedgers to mitigate potential losses resulting from adverse price movements in the underlying asset.
- **Speculation**: Traders can profit from both rising and falling markets by buying or selling futures contracts.
- **Leverage**: Futures trading involves a smaller initial investment (margin) compared to the notional value of the contract, allowing traders to control larger positions.

Futures Trading Strategies:

- **Long Position (Buying)**: A trader buys a futures contract with the expectation that the underlying asset's price will rise. If the price increases, the trader can sell the contract at a profit.
- **Short Position (Selling)**: A trader sells a futures contract with the expectation that the underlying asset's price will fall. If the price decreases, the trader can buy the contract back at a lower price, profiting from the difference.

- **Spread Trading**: Involves simultaneously taking both long and short positions in related futures contracts to profit from price differentials.
- **Hedging**: Corporations and producers use futures contracts to hedge against potential price fluctuations. For example, an oil producer might use futures contracts to lock in prices for future oil deliveries.

Futures Trading Process:

- **Select an Underlying Asset**: Choose the asset you want to trade, whether it's commodities like gold or agricultural products, stock indexes, currencies, or interest rates.
- **Choose a Futures Contract**: Select a specific futures contract based on the asset and its associated delivery date.
- **Place an Order**: Enter your buy or sell order with your brokerage. Specify the number of contracts and contract month.
- **Margin Requirements**: Pay the initial margin, which is a percentage of the contract's notional value. This margin ensures you have enough capital to cover potential losses.
- **Price Movements**: The contract's price will fluctuate based on market conditions. If the market moves in your favor, you can close the position for a profit.
- **Expiration and Settlement**: Futures contracts have expiration dates. On or before the expiration date, you can either close your position or allow it to settle, depending on the contract specifications.

Considerations and Risks:

- **Leverage and Risk**: While leverage allows for greater exposure, it also amplifies potential losses. It's important to manage risk through appropriate position sizing and risk management techniques.
- **Market Research**: In-depth research on the underlying asset's fundamentals and market trends is crucial for informed trading decisions.
- **Market Hours**: Futures markets have specific trading hours that may differ from regular stock markets.
- **Contract Specifications**: Each futures contract has unique specifications, including contract size, tick size, and expiration months.
- **Margin Calls**: If your account balance falls below the maintenance margin level, you may receive a margin call requiring additional funds.

Futures trading offers a range of opportunities for risk management, speculation, and profit potential. However, it also involves complexities and risks that require a solid understanding of the underlying assets, contract mechanics, and market dynamics. Before diving into futures trading, thorough education, practice, and risk management are essential. By approaching futures trading with discipline, strategy, and a comprehensive understanding of the markets, traders can navigate the derivatives landscape with confidence and work toward their trading objectives.

6.3 Margin Trading

Margin trading is a trading strategy that enables traders to amplify their potential gains by borrowing funds from a brokerage to increase their buying power. This practice allows traders to control larger positions than they could with their own capital alone. However, margin trading comes with increased risk, and traders must carefully manage their positions to avoid significant losses. This guide provides an overview of margin trading, its mechanics, benefits, risks, and considerations for those interested in utilizing margin as part of their trading strategy.

Understanding Margin Trading:

In margin trading, a trader borrows funds from a brokerage to increase their trading capital. This borrowed capital allows traders to take larger positions than they could afford with their own funds.

Key Terms:

- **Margin Account**: An account that allows traders to borrow funds for trading purposes. It's distinct from a cash account, which only contains the trader's own funds.
- **Initial Margin**: The amount of capital a trader must deposit to open a margin position. It's a percentage of the total position value.
- **Maintenance Margin**: The minimum account balance required to keep a margin position open. If the account balance falls below this level, a margin call may be triggered.

- **Margin Call**: A notification from the brokerage when the account's equity (account balance minus losses) falls below a certain threshold. Traders are required to deposit additional funds to bring the equity back above the maintenance margin.

Benefits of Margin Trading:

- **Increased Buying Power**: With borrowed funds, traders can control larger positions and potentially generate higher profits.
- **Diversification**: Margin trading allows traders to diversify their portfolios and access a broader range of assets.
- **Short Selling**: Traders can sell assets they don't own (short selling) with the intention of buying them back at a lower price.

Risks and Considerations:

- **Leverage Risk**: While leverage magnifies potential gains, it also increases potential losses. A small market movement can lead to significant losses.
- **Margin Calls**: Falling below the maintenance margin level triggers a margin call, requiring the trader to deposit additional funds to cover losses. Failure to do so could lead to the forced liquidation of positions.
- **Market Volatility**: Highly volatile markets can lead to rapid price movements that may result in margin calls.
- **Interest Costs**: Borrowed funds are subject to interest charges, which can erode profits if positions are held for extended periods.

- **Market Research**: In-depth research and analysis are essential to making informed trading decisions. Margin trading requires a deep understanding of the markets and the assets being traded.

Managing Risk in Margin Trading:

- **Position Sizing**: Calculate the appropriate position size based on your risk tolerance, account size, and trading strategy.
- **Stop-Loss Orders**: Set stop-loss orders to limit potential losses on each trade.
- **Risk-Reward Ratio**: Assess potential rewards against potential losses before entering a trade.

Margin trading can provide traders with opportunities to enhance their returns and access a broader range of assets. However, it's important to approach margin trading with caution, discipline, and a solid risk management strategy. Traders should fully understand the mechanics of margin accounts, the associated costs, and the risks involved. Leveraging borrowed funds amplifies both gains and losses, making it crucial to carefully assess your risk tolerance and trading strategy. By utilizing margin trading wisely and responsibly, traders can navigate the markets with a potential for increased profitability while minimizing the associated risks.

6.4 Short Selling

Short selling is a sophisticated trading strategy that allows traders to profit from falling prices in financial markets. Unlike traditional buying strategies, where traders aim to profit from price increases, short selling involves selling borrowed assets with the intention of buying them back at a lower price in the future. This strategy offers traders the opportunity to capitalize on market downturns, hedge against losses, and add diversity to their trading approach. This comprehensive guide delves into the intricacies of short selling, covering its mechanics, benefits, risks, strategies, and considerations for traders.

Understanding Short Selling:

In short selling, a trader borrows an asset (such as stocks, currencies, or commodities) from a broker and immediately sells it on the open market. The trader then aims to buy back the asset at a lower price, return it to the lender, and pocket the difference as profit.

Key Components of Short Selling:

- **Borrowing**: Traders borrow assets from brokers or other investors to facilitate the short sale.
- **Selling**: Traders sell the borrowed assets in the market, creating a short position.
- **Buying Back**: Traders monitor the market for price declines and buy back the assets at a lower price to close their short position.
- **Returning**: Traders return the borrowed assets to the lender, completing the short sale process.

Benefits of Short Selling:

- **Profit in Bear Markets**: Short selling allows traders to profit from declining markets, enabling them to capitalize on downward price trends.
- **Hedging**: Traders can use short selling as a hedge against losses in their long positions. If the market falls, the profits from short selling can offset losses in the long positions.
- **Diversification**: Short selling adds a new dimension to traders' portfolios by allowing them to profit from both upward and downward price movements.

Risks and Considerations:

- **Unlimited Loss Potential**: While the profit potential is limited to the asset's value, losses can be substantial if the asset's price rises significantly.
- **Borrowing Costs**: Borrowing assets may come with borrowing fees, which can impact potential profits.
- **Margin Calls**: If the shorted asset's price rises significantly, the broker may issue a margin call, requiring the trader to deposit additional funds to cover potential losses.

Short Selling Strategies:

- **Naked Short Selling**: Traders sell borrowed assets without already owning them. This strategy is subject to stringent regulations and is typically only available to certain institutional investors.

- **Covered Short Selling**: Traders sell borrowed assets but simultaneously hold a long position in another related asset. This strategy can help manage risk and mitigate losses.
- **Pairs Trading**: Traders simultaneously short an overvalued asset while longing for an undervalued asset in the same industry, sector, or market.
- **Event-Driven Short Selling**: Traders short-sell in anticipation of negative events, such as earnings disappointments, regulatory issues, or geopolitical uncertainties.

Mechanics of Short Selling:

- **Find a Borrower**: Traders must find a broker or another investor willing to lend them the assets they want to short.
- **Execute the Short Sale**: Traders sell the borrowed assets in the market, creating a short position.
- **Monitor the Market**: Traders track the asset's price movements, aiming to buy back the assets at a lower price.
- **Buy to Cover**: Traders buy back the assets at a lower price and return them to the lender, closing the short position.

Risk Management in Short Selling:

- **Set Stop-Loss Orders**: Determine price levels at which you will buy back the asset to limit potential losses.
- **Diversify**: Short selling should be part of a diversified trading strategy, and traders should avoid concentrating too much on a single short position.

Short selling is a valuable trading strategy that allows traders to profit from falling markets and potentially hedge against losses in their portfolios. However, it's a strategy that comes with significant risks and requires a deep understanding of market dynamics, regulations, and risk management techniques. Traders considering short selling should approach it with caution, discipline, and a thorough research process. By combining short selling with a well-rounded trading approach and sound risk management practices, traders can navigate both bull and bear markets with a more comprehensive toolkit and strive for success in the dynamic world of financial markets.

Chapter 7: Market Trends and News Analysis

In the world of finance, staying informed and making informed decisions is essential for successful trading and investment. Market trends and news analysis are powerful tools that traders and investors use to understand the ever-changing dynamics of financial markets, identify potential opportunities, and manage risk effectively. This comprehensive guide explores the significance of market trends and news analysis, their key components, methodologies, and practical applications for traders and investors seeking to navigate the complex world of finance.

Understanding Market Trends:

Market trends refer to the general direction in which a market or asset's price is moving over a period of time. Trends can be upward (bullish), downward (bearish), or sideways (neutral). Understanding market trends is critical for making informed trading decisions.

Types of Market Trends:

- **Uptrend (Bullish)**: Characterized by higher highs and higher lows, indicating a sustained upward movement in prices.
- **Downtrend (Bearish)**: Marked by lower highs and lower lows, reflecting a prolonged downward movement in prices.
- **Sideways Trend (Neutral or Range-bound)**: Prices move within a defined range without a clear upward or downward bias.

News Analysis and Its Impact:

News analysis involves examining current events, economic data releases, company announcements, geopolitical developments, and other relevant news to assess their potential impact on financial markets. News has the power to drive price movements and influence market sentiment.

Key Components of News Analysis:

- **Timeliness**: News that is released in real-time or shortly after an event occurs is often more impactful on market movements.
- **Relevance**: News related to economic indicators, corporate earnings, monetary policy decisions, and geopolitical events tends to have a significant impact.
- **Market Expectations**: Comparing actual news outcomes to market expectations can help assess the extent of the impact.

Market Trends and News Analysis: A Synergistic Approach:

- **Identification of Opportunities**: Combining market trends with news analysis can help traders identify opportunities aligning with the prevailing trend. For instance, a bullish trend coupled with positive economic data could suggest an opportunity for long positions.
- **Risk Management**: News events can introduce volatility and market uncertainty. Traders can adjust their risk management strategies to account for potential price fluctuations triggered by news releases.

- **Long-Term Investment Decisions**: Investors can analyze long-term market trends alongside macroeconomic indicators and news to make informed decisions about portfolio allocation and asset selection.

News Analysis Methodologies:

- **Fundamental Analysis**: Evaluating the impact of economic indicators, central bank decisions, corporate earnings reports, and geopolitical events on market trends.
- **Technical Analysis**: Using historical price and volume data to identify patterns and trends that can be influenced by news events.
- **Sentiment Analysis**: Assessing market sentiment by analyzing social media, news sentiment indicators, and options market data to gauge investor perceptions.

Practical Tips for Effective News Analysis:

- **Use Reliable Sources**: Rely on reputable news sources, financial news platforms, and official government or central bank statements for accurate information.
- **Stay Informed**: Regularly monitor news releases, economic calendars, and market commentary to stay up-to-date with relevant events.
- **Understand the Context**: Consider the broader economic and geopolitical context when interpreting news events' potential impact.
- **Be Objective**: Avoid emotional reactions to news events and assess their potential impact on market fundamentals and trends.

Risks and Challenges:

- **Market Volatility**: News events can lead to sharp price movements, making it essential to manage risk effectively.
- **Misinterpretation**: Incorrectly interpreting news events can lead to poor trading decisions. Therefore, thorough research is vital.

Market trends and news analysis are integral to successful trading and investment. By understanding prevailing market trends and analyzing news events' potential impact, traders and investors can make more informed decisions, capitalize on opportunities, and navigate market volatility with greater confidence. A combination of technical, fundamental, and sentiment analysis can provide a holistic view of the market environment. It's essential to approach news analysis with diligence, objectivity, and a commitment to ongoing learning to harness the power of information in the ever-evolving landscape of financial markets.

7.1 Staying Informed about Market Trends

In the fast-paced and ever-evolving world of finance, staying informed about market trends is paramount for traders and investors seeking to make informed decisions and navigate the complexities of financial markets. Market trends provide valuable insights into the direction of prices, helping traders identify potential opportunities and manage risks effectively. This guide outlines practical strategies and resources for staying informed about market trends, allowing individuals to enhance their trading and investment strategies with up-to-date information and insights.

1. **Utilize Reliable News Sources:**

- **Reputable Financial News Websites**: Trusted financial news websites such as Bloomberg, CNBC, Reuters, and Financial Times provide real-time updates, analysis, and expert opinions on various asset classes and market sectors.
- **Official Government and Central Bank Releases**: Direct information from government agencies, central banks, and regulatory bodies can provide crucial insights into economic data, monetary policy decisions, and regulatory changes.

2. **Follow Economic Calendars:**

Economic calendars provide schedules of upcoming economic releases, such as employment reports, GDP figures, inflation data, and interest rate decisions. Websites like ForexFactory and Investing.com offer comprehensive economic calendars that help traders anticipate market-moving events.

3. **Leverage Market Analysis Platforms:**

- **Technical Analysis Platforms**: Platforms like TradingView offer technical analysis tools, charts, and indicators that help traders identify trends and potential turning points based on historical price data.
- **Fundamental Analysis Platforms**: Platforms like Seeking Alpha and Yahoo Finance provide comprehensive company profiles,

earnings reports, and fundamental data for making informed investment decisions.

4. Social Media and Financial Blogs:

Follow financial experts, analysts, and reputable financial bloggers on social media platforms such as Twitter and LinkedIn. Many professionals share insights, market commentary, and news updates in real-time.

5. News Aggregator Apps:

Download news aggregator apps that curate and deliver news updates from various sources in one place. Apps like Flipboard and Feedly allow you to customize your news feed based on your interests.

6. Podcasts and Webinars:

Listen to financial podcasts and webinars hosted by industry experts. These platforms often cover market trends, investment strategies, and emerging opportunities.

7. Analyze Market Sentiment:

Monitor sentiment indicators like the Volatility Index (VIX), which reflects investor fear and market volatility. Additionally, sentiment analysis tools can gauge social media discussions and news sentiment to understand market sentiment shifts.

8.   Join Online Trading Communities:

Participate in online trading communities, forums, and discussion groups. Engaging with other traders and investors can provide diverse perspectives and insights into market trends.

9.   Attend Seminars and Conferences:

Participate in seminars, workshops, and financial conferences to hear from experts, learn about emerging trends, and gain new perspectives on market dynamics.

10. Stay Abreast of Global Developments:

Understand the potential impact of geopolitical events, economic policies, and global trends on financial markets. Being aware of global developments can help you anticipate market reactions.

11. Set Alerts and Notifications:

Utilize email alerts, mobile apps, and trading platforms to receive notifications for important news releases and market movements.

12. Create a Routine:

Develop a daily routine to review market news and updates. Set aside dedicated time to stay informed and make informed trading decisions.

Staying informed about market trends is a continuous and essential process for traders and investors. A combination of reliable news sources, economic calendars, analysis platforms, social media engagement, and participation in trading communities can help you gather a comprehensive view of the market landscape. By dedicating time to stay informed and utilizing a variety of resources, you can enhance your ability to identify opportunities, manage risks, and make well-informed trading and investment decisions in the dynamic and rapidly changing world of finance.

7.2 Impact of News on Stock Prices

News plays a pivotal role in shaping the behavior of financial markets and influencing stock prices. Whether it's corporate earnings announcements, economic data releases, geopolitical events, or regulatory developments, news has the power to trigger significant price movements and shape investor sentiment. Understanding the intricate relationship between news and stock prices is essential for traders and investors seeking to navigate the complexities of the market. This guide explores the profound impact of news on stock prices, its underlying mechanisms, and strategies to capitalize on its effects.

The Relationship Between News and Stock Prices:

- **Immediate Reaction**: News releases often lead to immediate reactions in stock prices. Positive news can drive prices higher, while negative news can lead to declines.
- **Market Sentiment**: News influences investor sentiment, which in turn affects buying and selling decisions. Positive news boosts optimism, while negative news fosters caution.
- **Price Volatility**: News can introduce volatility as investors react to new information. Volatility can be both an opportunity and a risk for traders.

Types of News Affecting Stock Prices:

- **Earnings Reports**: Companies' quarterly and annual earnings reports provide insights into their financial health and performance. Strong earnings growth typically leads to price increases, while poor earnings can lead to declines.
- **Economic Indicators**: Economic data releases, such as employment reports, GDP figures, and inflation data, can impact stock prices by influencing investor expectations about economic growth.
- **Mergers and Acquisitions**: News of mergers, acquisitions, and takeovers can lead to price changes in the involved companies' stocks.
- **Regulatory and Legal Developments**: News related to regulatory changes, legal disputes, or government actions can impact stock prices, particularly in industries directly affected by such news.

- **Geopolitical Events**: Political events, international conflicts, and geopolitical developments can lead to market uncertainty and impact stock prices.

Mechanisms of News Impact:

- **Efficient Market Hypothesis (EMH)**: The EMH suggests that all available information is instantly priced into stocks, implying that market prices reflect news immediately.
- **Overreaction and Correction**: In some cases, markets may overreact to news, causing exaggerated price movements. Subsequently, prices may be corrected as new information is digested.
- **Delayed Reaction**: Inefficient markets or news with complex implications might lead to delayed price adjustments as investors gradually process the information.

Strategies to Navigate News Impact:

- **Preparation**: Stay informed about upcoming news releases and events to anticipate potential price movements.
- **Risk Management**: Implement appropriate risk management strategies to safeguard against unexpected price swings.
- **Volatility Strategies**: Use options or volatility-based trading strategies to profit from increased price volatility during news events.
- **Contrarian Approach**: If news causes a market overreaction, consider taking contrarian positions if you believe prices will eventually revert to their true value.

- **Trend Following**: If news confirms an existing trend, consider trend-following strategies that capitalize on the continuation of the price movement.
- **News Trading**: Execute trades immediately after news releases to capture short-term price movements.

Challenges and Considerations:

- **Market Noise**: Not all news is equally impactful; discerning between noise and significant news is crucial.
- **Timing**: Executing trades immediately after news releases can be challenging due to price volatility and slippage.
- **False Signals**: News events can sometimes lead to false signals, causing price reversals shortly after the initial movement.

News is a driving force behind stock price movements, shaping market sentiment, volatility, and investment decisions. Understanding the impact of different types of news on stock prices and employing suitable trading strategies can empower traders and investors to navigate markets effectively. By staying informed, adapting to market reactions, and implementing sound risk management, individuals can leverage the power of news to their advantage and make informed trading decisions in the dynamic world of financial markets.

7.3 Using News Wisely in Trading

News is a valuable tool that traders can harness to inform their decisions, capitalize on opportunities, and manage risk effectively. However, the abundance of information, the speed of news dissemination, and the potential for misinformation can make using news in trading a challenge. Employing a thoughtful and strategic approach is essential to ensure that news becomes a powerful asset rather than a source of confusion. This guide delves into strategies for using news wisely in trading, helping traders make informed decisions amidst the dynamic and information-rich world of financial markets.

1. Validate News Sources:

Not all sources are reliable or unbiased. Rely on reputable financial news platforms, official government releases, and established financial research organizations for accurate and credible information.

2. Prioritize Relevance:

Filter news according to its relevance to your trading strategy and the assets you are trading. Focus on news that directly impacts the markets you are interested in.

3. Understand the Context:

Consider the broader economic, geopolitical, and industrial context surrounding news events. News can have varying impacts depending on the broader landscape.

4. Distinguish Between Fact and Opinion:

Differentiate between factual news reports and opinion pieces. While both can provide insights, opinions should be considered alongside other objective information.

5. Analyze Market Expectations:

Compare news outcomes to market expectations. Positive news may not lead to price increases if the market is already anticipating it. Deviations from expectations can be more impactful.

6. Consider the Time Horizon:

News can have short-term or long-term effects. Determine whether a news event is likely to cause short-lived volatility or lead to a sustained price trend.

7. Use Multiple Sources:

Cross-reference news from multiple sources to verify accuracy and ensure a comprehensive understanding of the event's implications.

8. Avoid Emotional Reactions:

Emotional reactions to news events can lead to impulsive trading decisions. Maintain a disciplined approach and base decisions on analysis rather than emotions.

9. Manage Risk:

Consider how news might impact your existing positions and risk exposure. Implement risk management techniques to mitigate potential losses during periods of high volatility.

10. Diversify Information Channels:

Explore a variety of information sources, including financial news websites, social media, podcasts, and expert analysis. Each channel can provide unique insights.

11. Focus on Key Events:

Prioritize major economic releases, central bank decisions, earnings reports, and significant geopolitical events that are likely to have a notable impact on markets.

12. Avoid Overtrading:

Not every news event requires immediate action. Overtrading in response to every piece of news can lead to impulsive decisions and increased transaction costs.

13. Backtest News-Based Strategies:

If employing news-based trading strategies, backtest them to assess their historical performance and refine their parameters.

14. Be Patient:

Sometimes the most prudent course of action is to wait for news-related volatility to subside before making trading decisions.

15. Continuous Learning:

Stay updated on changes in market behavior and the impact of news over time. The markets evolve, and strategies need to adapt accordingly.

News can be a valuable asset for traders when used wisely. By validating sources, focusing on relevance, considering context, and implementing strategic approaches, traders can make informed decisions that align with their trading objectives. Remember that using news effectively requires a blend of critical thinking, discipline, and continuous learning. As you refine your ability to interpret and leverage news, you can navigate the markets with greater confidence and make trading decisions that are grounded in a well-informed perspective.

Chapter 8: Continuous Learning and Improvement

In the ever-evolving landscape of trading and investing, the pursuit of continuous learning and improvement is not just a choice; it's a necessity. Whether you're a novice trader seeking to build a strong foundation or an experienced investor looking to refine your strategies, the commitment to lifelong learning is key to staying ahead in a dynamic and competitive field. This comprehensive guide explores the significance of continuous learning, strategies for ongoing improvement, and the transformative impact it can have on traders and investors striving for mastery.

The Power of Continuous Learning:

- **Adaptation to Market Changes**: Markets are influenced by various factors, including technological advancements, economic shifts, and regulatory changes. Continuous learning equips you with the tools to adapt to these changes.
- **Skill Refinement**: Through continuous learning, traders refine their analytical skills, risk management techniques, and decision-making processes, leading to more effective trading strategies.
- **Informed Decision-Making**: Ongoing education ensures you are well informed about market trends, economic indicators, and industry developments, enabling better decision-making.

Strategies for Continuous Learning and Improvement:

1. **Formal Education:**

Enroll in courses, seminars, workshops, and webinars offered by educational institutions, trading platforms, and financial organizations. Formal education provides structured learning and in-depth knowledge.

2. Self-Directed Learning:

Leverage online resources, books, articles, and research papers to deepen your understanding of trading concepts, market trends, and investment strategies.

3. Mentorship:

Seek guidance from experienced traders, investors, or mentors who can provide personalized insights, share their experiences, and offer constructive feedback.

4. Virtual Trading and Simulation:

Utilize virtual trading platforms to practice trading strategies without risking real capital. Simulated trading allows you to test and refine your approaches in a risk-free environment.

5. Stay Updated:

Regularly follow financial news, subscribe to market analysis newsletters, and engage with industry-related content on social media platforms.

6. Peer Networking:

Connect with fellow traders and investors to exchange ideas, strategies, and insights. Peer networking provides diverse perspectives and opportunities for collaboration.

7. Reflect and Analyze:

Review your trades, successes, and failures. Identify patterns, analyze mistakes, and derive lessons to improve your trading approach.

8. Set Goals:

Establish short-term and long-term learning goals. Setting goals gives your learning journey direction and purpose.

9. Psychological Growth:

Continuous learning extends beyond technical aspects. Enhance your emotional intelligence, discipline, and psychological resilience to navigate the mental challenges of trading.

10. Experiment and Innovate:

Explore new trading strategies, test unconventional approaches, and adapt to changing market conditions. Innovation often leads to valuable insights.

11. Embrace Technology:

Stay updated with technological advancements and tools that can enhance your trading efficiency and analytical capabilities.

12. Document Your Journey:

Maintain a trading journal where you record your trades, strategies, observations, and emotional experiences. This documentation fosters self-awareness and learning.

The Transformative Impact of Continuous Learning:

- **Confidence**: Continuous learning equips you with knowledge, fostering self-assuredness in your trading decisions.
- **Adaptability**: As markets evolve, your capacity to adapt to new trends, technologies, and strategies becomes a competitive advantage.
- **Risk Management**: Learning from mistakes and refining your approach reduces the likelihood of costly errors.

- **Innovation**: Ongoing education encourages innovation, enabling you to explore creative strategies and refine existing ones.
- **Long-Term Success**: Mastery in trading and investing requires a commitment to continuous improvement. The journey is ongoing, but the rewards are enduring.

Overcoming Challenges:

- **Time Management**: Allocate dedicated time for learning amidst your trading activities. Even small, consistent efforts can yield substantial results.
- **Information Overload**: Focus on quality over quantity. Filter information to prioritize what's relevant to your trading goals.

Continuous learning and improvement form the bedrock of successful trading and investing. By cultivating a mindset of curiosity, resilience, and adaptability, traders and investors position themselves for long-term success. The trading landscape is characterized by its complexities and uncertainties, but the commitment to learning empowers individuals to navigate these challenges with confidence and skill. Embrace learning as an integral part of your journey, and you'll not only sharpen your trading acumen but also unlock the limitless potential for growth and mastery in the dynamic world of finance.

8.1 Reviewing and Adapting Strategies

In the ever-changing realm of trading and investing, the ability to review, adapt, and refine strategies is a critical component of achieving consistent success. Markets evolve, economic conditions shift, and unforeseen events occur, making it essential for traders and investors to regularly assess their approaches and make necessary adjustments. This guide delves into the significance of reviewing and adapting strategies, the methodologies involved, and the transformative impact this practice can have on optimizing trading and investment outcomes.

The Importance of Strategy Review and Adaptation:

- **Market Dynamics**: Markets are influenced by a multitude of factors that can alter the effectiveness of strategies over time. Regular review ensures alignment with current market conditions.
- **Continuous Improvement**: Strategies can always be refined, enhanced, or adapted to account for new insights, technologies, and opportunities.
- **Risk Management**: Reviewing and adapting strategies allows traders and investors to mitigate risks by addressing weaknesses or vulnerabilities in their approach.

Methodologies for Strategy Review and Adaptation:

1. Regular Performance Evaluation:

Conduct frequent assessments of your trading or investment performance. Analyze both winning and losing trades to identify patterns, strengths, and areas for improvement.

2. Statistical Analysis:

Utilize statistical tools to measure the success rate, risk-to-reward ratios, and other relevant metrics of your strategies. This data-driven approach provides objective insights.

3. Backtesting:

Backtest your strategies using historical data to assess their performance under different market conditions. This helps you identify potential shortcomings and refine your approach.

4. Real-time Monitoring:

Monitor the performance of your strategies in real-time. This allows you to detect deviations and adjust your approach promptly.

5. Journaling:

Maintain a detailed trading journal where you record your decisions, rationale, emotions, and outcomes. This self-analysis aids in identifying patterns and emotional biases.

6. Peer and Mentor Feedback:

Engage with fellow traders, investors, or mentors to gain external perspectives on your strategies. Their insights can shed light on blind spots.

7. Psychological Assessment:

Evaluate your emotional responses to losses, gains, and market volatility. Emotional discipline is integral to strategy effectiveness.

Adapting Strategies for Optimal Outcomes:

1. Stay Open to Change:

Embrace the reality that strategies may need to evolve over time. Be willing to challenge existing beliefs and experiment with new approaches.

2. Identify Weaknesses:

Pinpoint areas of your strategy that consistently yield unfavorable outcomes. These weak points need to be addressed to enhance performance.

3. Analyze Trends and Data:

Leverage historical and current market data to identify changing trends and dynamics that might necessitate strategy adjustments.

4. Market Research:

Stay informed about market trends, economic indicators, and industry developments to anticipate changes that could impact your strategies.

5. Flexibility in Execution:

Adapt your execution to align with the prevailing market conditions. This could involve adjusting position sizes, entry/exit points, or time frames.

6. Incremental Changes:

Make gradual adjustments to your strategies rather than wholesale changes. This allows you to assess the impact of modifications more effectively.

7. Simulate and Test:

Before fully implementing changes, test adaptations using simulation or paper trading to evaluate their impact in a risk-free environment.

The Transformative Impact:

- **Enhanced Consistency**: Adapted strategies are more likely to deliver consistent results across varying market conditions.
- **Mitigated Drawdowns**: Addressing weaknesses and vulnerabilities in your strategies can help prevent significant losses during unfavorable market phases.
- **Increased Resilience**: Adaptive strategies are better equipped to withstand unexpected events and market shocks.

Challenges and Considerations:

- **Over-Optimization**: Avoid excessively modifying strategies based on historical data to prevent overfitting to past market conditions.
- **Patience and Persistence**: Not all adaptations lead to instant success. Patience is required to assess the long-term impact.

Reviewing and adapting strategies is a hallmark of successful traders and investors. In a landscape characterized by volatility and uncertainty, the ability to pivot, optimize, and refine approaches is a source of competitive advantage. The practice of continuous improvement ensures that strategies remain aligned with evolving market realities, leading to more consistent outcomes and greater long-term success. Embrace the iterative nature of strategy development, and you'll find that the journey of adaptation is a dynamic process that enhances your ability to navigate the complex world of trading and investment.

8.2 Learning from Mistakes and Successes

In the dynamic realm of trading and investing, the journey toward mastery is paved with both successes and failures. Learning from these experiences is a fundamental aspect of growth and improvement. Every trade executed, whether profitable or not, offers valuable insights that can refine strategies, enhance decision-making, and ultimately contribute to long-term success. This guide explores the profound impact of learning from mistakes and successes, strategies for effective reflection, and the transformative role it plays in traders' and investors' journeys toward mastery.

The Significance of Learning from Mistakes and Successes:

- **Self-Awareness**: Reflecting on both mistakes and successes fosters self-awareness, helping traders and investors recognize their strengths and areas for improvement.
- **Continuous Improvement**: By analyzing outcomes, traders can refine strategies, refine risk management techniques, and adapt their approaches for better performance.
- **Resilience**: Learning from failures and overcoming challenges cultivates emotional resilience, a vital trait in navigating the ups and downs of financial markets.

Strategies for Learning from Mistakes:

1. Identify the Cause:

Dive deep into your trading mistakes to understand the root causes. Was it a misjudgment of market trends, poor timing, or overleveraging? Pinpoint the factors that contributed to the error.

2. Maintain a Trading Journal:

Record each trade, along with the rationale behind your decisions. Documenting emotions, thoughts, and outcomes provides valuable material for analysis.

3. Review Losing Trades:

Periodically review losing trades and examine what went wrong. Did you adhere to your strategy? Were there external factors that influenced the outcome?

4. Accept Responsibility:

Accept accountability for your mistakes. Blaming external factors hinders growth. Embrace your role in the outcome and focus on learning.

5. Extract Lessons:

Every mistake offers a lesson. Whether it's about risk management, market analysis, or psychological discipline, seek to extract actionable insights.

Strategies for Learning from Successes:

1. Analyze Winning Trades:

Just as you review losing trades, analyze your winning trades. Identify what worked well in your strategy and why the trade succeeded.

2. Avoid Overconfidence:

While celebrating successes is natural, avoid becoming overconfident. Remember that market conditions can change, and past successes may not always be replicated.

3. Identify Patterns:

Identify patterns and strategies that consistently lead to success. Incorporate these elements into your trading approach to increase your chances of positive outcomes.

4. Reinforce Good Habits:

Positive outcomes often result from adhering to disciplined strategies. Reinforce these good habits to maintain consistency.

The Transformative Impact:

- **Refined Decision-Making**: Learning from both mistakes and successes fine-tunes your decision-making process, enabling you to make more informed choices.
- **Adaptation**: Insights gained from experiences guide you in adapting strategies to evolving market conditions and refining your approach.
- **Psychological Growth**: Overcoming mistakes and celebrating successes contribute to emotional resilience, improving your ability to manage market volatility.

Challenges and Considerations:

- **Emotional Detachment**: Learning from mistakes and successes requires emotional detachment. Analyze objectively without letting emotions cloud your judgment.
- **Time Frame**: Some lessons take time to reveal themselves. Be patient and don't rush the process of learning and adaptation.

Learning from mistakes and successes is an essential aspect of becoming a proficient trader or investor. By embracing failures as learning opportunities and understanding the factors contributing to successes, you build a foundation for continuous improvement. The journey toward mastery is marked by a commitment to self-reflection, the ability to adapt, and the humility to acknowledge that growth comes from both triumphs and setbacks. As you navigate the complexities of financial markets, remember that each experience, whether a gain or a loss, is a stepping stone on your path to becoming a more skilled and resilient participant in the world of trading and investing.

8.3 Seeking Ongoing Education

In the dynamic world of trading and investing, the pursuit of ongoing education is a driving force behind continuous growth and lasting success. As markets evolve, new strategies emerge, and economic landscapes change, traders and investors who commit to learning remain at the forefront of innovation and adaptability. This guide explores the profound impact of seeking ongoing education, strategies for effective learning, and the transformative role it plays in shaping the journeys of individuals striving for excellence in trading and investing.

The Value of Ongoing Education:

- **Adaptation to Changing Markets**: Markets are influenced by evolving trends, technologies, and economic conditions. Ongoing education equips traders with the tools to adapt their strategies accordingly.
- **Enhanced Decision-Making**: A well-informed trader is better equipped to make sound decisions rooted in a deep understanding of market dynamics.

- **Exploration of New Opportunities**: Continuous learning exposes traders to innovative strategies, asset classes, and investment vehicles, expanding their toolkit.

Strategies for Effective Ongoing Education:

1. Formal Courses:

Enroll in courses, workshops, and seminars offered by reputable institutions and industry experts. Formal education provides structured learning and comprehensive insights.

2. Online Learning Platforms:

Leverage online platforms that offer a wide range of courses, webinars, and tutorials on trading strategies, technical analysis, and market trends.

3. Mentorship:

Seek guidance from experienced traders or investors who can offer personalized insights, real-world experiences, and valuable feedback.

4. Financial Literature:

Read books, articles, research papers, and industry publications to gain in-depth knowledge about trading concepts and investment strategies.

5. Attend Conferences and Seminars:

Participate in financial conferences, seminars, and workshops to learn from industry experts, network with peers, and stay updated on market trends.

6. Online Communities:

Engage with online trading communities, forums, and social media groups to share insights, ask questions, and learn from the experiences of fellow traders.

7. Analyze Market Trends:

Stay informed about economic indicators, geopolitical events, and industry developments to anticipate market trends and opportunities.

8. Experiment with New Strategies:

Allocate time to test and experiment with new trading strategies in a controlled environment to gain practical experience.

The Transformative Impact:

- **Holistic Understanding**: Ongoing education provides a well-rounded understanding of trading and investing, encompassing technical, fundamental, and psychological aspects.
- **Innovation**: Learning about emerging technologies, trading platforms, and investment vehicles empowers traders to innovate and stay competitive.
- **Confidence**: Knowledge gained through education instills confidence in decision-making and the ability to navigate complex market scenarios.

Challenges and Considerations:

- **Information Overload**: With a plethora of information available, focus on quality over quantity. Prioritize information that aligns with your trading goals.
- **Time Management**: Allocate dedicated time for learning amidst your trading activities. The balance between execution and education is crucial.

Ongoing education is the foundation of sustained success in trading and investing. Embrace learning as a continuous journey rather than a destination. By seeking knowledge from diverse sources, adapting to new insights, and continuously refining your skills, you position yourself as a knowledgeable and adaptable participant in the dynamic world of finance. Remember that learning is not just about acquiring facts; it's about cultivating a mindset of growth, curiosity, and resilience that drives you to excel in your trading and investment endeavors.

Conclusion

In the intricate world of stock trading, where opportunities and challenges coexist, the journey to profitability demands a solid foundation of knowledge and the unwavering confidence to navigate market dynamics. "Profitable Strategies: A Comprehensive Guide to Understanding the Fundamentals of Stock Trading" has been your roadmap to acquiring the skills, insights, and strategies necessary to thrive in the competitive landscape of the stock market.

Throughout this guide, we've delved deep into the essentials, beginning with the importance of understanding market fundamentals. From comprehending the intricacies of stocks and market operations to deciphering economic indicators and mastering various trading techniques, you've been equipped with a wealth of information. You've gained insights into both technical and fundamental analyses, and learned about trading psychology, risk management, and the art of developing disciplined mindsets.

The significance of continuous learning, honing strategies, and learning from both mistakes and successes has been underscored. By embracing the power of news, understanding market trends, and seeking ongoing education, you've discovered how to stay informed and adaptable in the ever-changing trading landscape.

In the quest for profitable trading, remember that success is not an endpoint but a journey. Every chapter, every strategy, and every insight you've gained is a stepping stone toward refining your approach, enhancing your decision-making, and ultimately achieving your financial goals. The road to profitability is marked by dedication, perseverance, and a commitment to self-improvement.

As you venture into the world of stock trading armed with knowledge and confidence, remember that every trade is an opportunity to learn, adapt, and grow. The market's unpredictability may present challenges, but with the skills and insights you've acquired, you're better prepared to navigate them.

Profitable trading isn't just about monetary gains; it's about the empowerment that comes from understanding the intricacies of the market, making informed decisions, and building a sustainable approach to wealth creation. With the principles and strategies you've explored, you're poised to make your mark in the world of stock trading, armed with the tools to harness opportunities and overcome obstacles.

In closing, remember that the journey of profitable trading is an ongoing one. Markets will ebb and flow, trends will shift, and challenges will arise. But armed with the knowledge, confidence, and insights you've gained from this comprehensive guide, you're well-equipped to tackle whatever comes your way and embark on a journey of continuous growth, success, and financial achievement in the captivating realm of stock trading.